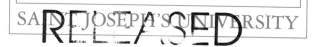

THE UNIVERSITY OF MICHIGAN
CENTER FOR JAPANESE STUDIES

MICHIGAN PAPERS IN JAPANESE STUDIES
NO. 14

MICHIGAN PAPERS IN JAPANESE STUDIES

No. 2. *Parties, Candidates, and Voters in Japan: Six Quantitative Studies*, edited by John Creighton Campbell.

No. 3. *The Japanese Automobile Industry: Model and Challenge for the Future*, edited by Robert E. Cole.

No. 4. *Survey of Japanese Collections in the United States, 1979-1980*, by Naomi Fukuda.

No. 5. *Culture and Religion in Japanese-American Relations: Essays on Uchimura Kanzō, 1861-1930*, edited by Ray A. Moore.

No. 6. *Sukeroku's Double Identity: The Dramatic Structure of Edo Kabuki*, by Barbara E. Thornbury.

No. 7. *Industry at the Crossroads*, edited by Robert E. Cole.

No. 8. *Treelike: The Poetry of Kinoshita Yūji*, translated by Robert Epp.

No. 9. *The New Religions of Japan: A Bibliography of Western-Language Materials*, 2nd ed., by H. Byron Earhart.

No. 10. *Automobiles and the Future: Competition, Cooperation, and Change*, edited by Robert E. Cole.

No. 11. *Collective Decision Making in Rural Japan*, by Robert C. Marshall.

No. 12. *"The Sting of Death" and Other Stories*, by Shimao Toshio. Translated by Kathryn Sparling.

No. 13. *The American Automobile Industry: Rebirth or Requiem?*, edited by Robert E. Cole.

No. 14. *Entrepreneurship in a "Mature Industry"*, edited by John Creighton Campbell.

Entrepreneurship in a "Mature Industry"

edited by

John Creighton Campbell

Ann Arbor

Center for Japanese Studies
The University of Michigan

1986

ISBN 0-939512-22-X

Copyright 1986

Center for Japanese Studies
The University of Michigan
108 Lane Hall
Ann Arbor, MI 48109

Cover design by Eric Ernst

Library of Congress Cataloging in Publication Data

Main entry under title:

Entrepreneurship in a "mature industry".

(Michigan papers in Japanese studies; no. 14)
Proceedings of the 5th U.S.-Japan Automotive Industry Confer-
ence, held at the University of Michigan in Mar. 1985.
Includes bibliographies.
1. Automobile industry and trade— Management—Congresses. 2.
Automobile   industry   and   trade—United   States—
Management—Congresses.   3.   Automobile   industry   and
trade—Japan— Management— Congresses.
I. Campbell, John Creighton. II. University of Michigan. Center for
Japanese Studies. III. U.S.-Japan Automotive Industry Conference
(5th : 1985 : University of Michigan). IV. Series.
HD9710.A2E58   1985   338.4'76292   85-29128
ISBN 0-939512-22-X

Contents

Part 1: Public Forum

Part 2: Issues for Debate

Contributors

JOHN CREIGHTON CAMPBELL is Associate Professor of Political Science and Director of the Center for Japanese Studies, The University of Michigan.

EDMUND M. CARPENTER is the Vice President of ITT and the President and Chief Executive Officer of ITT Industrial Technology Corporation.

ROBERT E. COLE is Professor of Sociology and Business Administration at the University of Michigan.

DONALD EPHLIN is International Vice President and Director of the General Motors Department, United Automobile Workers.

SHOICHIRO IRIMAJIRI is President of Honda of America Manufacturing.

DANIEL T. JONES is Senior Research Fellow of the Science Policy Research Unit, The University of Sussex. He was the U.K. team leader for MIT's Future of the Automobile Program.

ROSABETH MOSS KANTER is Professor of Sociology and Organization and Management at Yale University and Chairman of the Board of Goodmeasure, Inc., a Boston-based management consulting firm.

PAUL W. MCCRACKEN is Edmund Ezra Day Distinguished University Professor of Business Administration, The University of Michigan.

F. JAMES MCDONALD is President of General Motors Corporation.

VLADIMIR PUCIK is Assistant Professor of International Business, the Graduate School of Business, The University of Michigan.

TAIZO YAKUSHIJI is an Associate Professor at the Graduate Institute of Policy Science, The University of Saitama, and an ACLS Fellow at the Berkeley Roundtable on International Economy at the University of California, Berkeley.

Preface

The fifth annual U.S.-Japan Automotive Industry Conference was held in March 1985, shortly after the Reagan administration decided not to ask Japan to renew the Voluntary Restraint Agreement on auto exports. Our conferences had chronicled four eventful years: the onslaught of Japanese small cars and of so many lessons from Japan, economic recession and recovery, the resuscitation of Chrysler, the arrival of Japanese firms on our shores, and enormous new investment by the American auto industry.

This year, the conference organizing committee decided to step back a pace from the events of the moment, engrossing as these were, to focus on a single theme. Arguably the most important impact of the Japanese challenge to Detroit was a sudden loss of complacency, a realization that the old ways would no longer be enough. A "mature" industry was suddenly thrust back into adolescence. The response was a surge of entrepreneurial behavior, not just the individual flamboyance of a Lee Iacocca, but a host of innovations in product, manufacturing, internal organization, and relationships between OEMs and suppliers. This new attention to entrepreneurship certainly continues today, as it must if the American industry is to prosper in the face of inevitably intensifying competition from Japanese companies, not to mention the Koreans and perhaps others.

We became a bit entrepreneurial ourselves in planning the conference: for the first time we invited an outsider to the auto industry as our keynote speaker. Since leaving the Ann Arbor campus with a Ph.D. in 1967, Rosabeth Kanter has become well known in both the academic and managerial worlds for her research on organizational innovation. The first version of her presentation was circulated to the other forum speakers so they could react to her ideas, which were just as provocative as we had hoped. Moreover, we could hardly do better than to present F. James McDonald, the president of General Motors—then in the midst of planning Saturn and the soon-to-be-announced acquisition of Electronic Data Systems—and Shoichiro Irimajiri, the president of Honda of America Manufacturing—the first Japanese auto firm to undertake large-scale manufacturing in the U.S., as it has been first in so many other areas. The program was rounded out by Edmund Carpenter and Donald Ephlin, who are uniquely able to discuss entrepreneurship both as individuals and as representatives of distinctly innovative organizations in the parts supply and labor fields.

All the speakers' complete speeches from the forum are presented in this volume—more than complete in Ms. Kanter's case, since she kindly provided us with a complete original article on how entrepreneurship can work in practice. Paul McCracken's evening speech, which aroused subsequent comment for his personal challenge to Japan, is also included.

Finally, continuing a practice we started last year, three additional essays have been added. These are: a revised version of a provocative talk given by Taizo Yakushiji at the U.S.-Japan Forum; an article by Vladimir Pucik on white-collar personnel in the U.S. and Japanese auto industries that grew out of his research for the Joint U.S.-Japan Automotive Industry Study; and a discussion of world automotive trends by Daniel Jones, originally prepared for the first meeting of the International Automotive Forum at Hakone, Japan, in November 1984. We are delighted to make these important articles available to a broader audience.

When I came to Ann Arbor in 1972 as a specialist in Japanese politics, I certainly did not expect to be organizing a conference of hundreds of executives about the auto industry. I am not sure whether such new experiences keep people young or age them prematurely. Our conference coordinator, Lorraine Sobson, no doubt wonders the same, but she did a terrific job, as did the associate coordinator, John Voorhorst, and the legions of students who helped out. Thanks are due as well to the staff of the Center for Japanese Studies, especially Elsie Orb, who handled the finances and much else; Bruce E. Willoughby, who edited this volume as expertly as always; and Catherine Arnott, who kept the computers humming. Downs Herold and Pat Rapley of the Industrial Development Division provided many suggestions and much help with mailing lists, and Joan Eadie and the staff of Conferences and Institutes did a fine job with registrations. As a neophyte organizer, I owe special thanks to the always solid advice and hard work of the conference steering committee, including David Cole, Vladimir Pucik, Don Smith, and especially my predecessor Robert Cole, who with a minimum of arm-twisting agreed both to moderate the conference and to organize an excellent workshop. My utmost thanks must go to the forum speakers and to those who organized and participated in the ten workshops on the second day. It is impressive that so many people could be so interesting.

John Campbell
Director, Center for Japanese Studies
Associate Professor of Political Science
The University of Michigan

PART I: PUBLIC FORUM

Opening Statement

Robert E. Cole

For the last four years my job was primarily to serve as organizer of the auto conference. At this point every year I would take a deep breath, relax, and enjoy watching that smoothie Paul McCracken take over. This year, I thought I had escaped entirely. I was in Washington and John Campbell, the director of the Center for Japanese Studies, had taken over the prime responsibility for organizing the conference. But Paul ended up as the evening speaker, and, as you see, I ended up not being able to relax and enjoy the proceedings. The moral of the story, naturally, is never to underestimate the wiles of a conservative.

When John Campbell indicated that the theme for this year was "Entrepreneurship in a Mature Industry," I thought that it was a pretty good choice in light of what I saw happening in the industry. And when he told me later that the keynote speaker was Rosabeth Kanter, I began to think we had the makings for a really excellent set of discussions. Then I learned that we would have with us Mr. Irimajiri of Honda, the Japanese auto firm most noted for its entrepreneurial spirit; that provided further reinforcement. And still later, as the newspapers were flooded with Saturns and EDSs, I concluded that it was a stroke of genius. We will have a chance to see shortly if my judgments are correct.

As a way of raising some questions about our topic, I would like to make some observations on the concept of entrepreneurship. There is a way in which, at any one time, a set of concepts capture the attention of business leaders as keys to economic success. Organizational culture, excellence, quality, and entrepreneurship are some of the more fashionable concepts today.

And there is always a tendency on the part of some to take such a concept as entrepreneurship and make it appear that it is the

1

be-all and end-all of success. Indeed, what is capitalism in its most
pristine form but entrepreneurship; so, one might reason that it
must lie at the heart of the economic success of individual firms. This
is particularly the case in the auto industry where there are — as
many have pointed out — strong signs of a dematuration process
taking place. Clearly the internationalization of the industry and the
lack of certainty as to process and product technology, competitive
relationships, employment, and union-management relationships
represent profound alterations of the industry over the last ten
years.

To what extent is entrepreneurship key to the survival of
given firms and constituencies? I hope we will move toward some
clarity on that matter today and tomorrow. But I would point out
now that entrepreneurship can mean many things to many people.
It can mean bringing in 300,000 Korean and Japanese cars by
American auto firms — so that they become primarily distributors at
the small-car end of the market. And what does that mean for the
jobs of U.S. engineers, managers, and production workers? It can
mean moving out of the auto industry to new ventures, as did U.S.
Steel with Marathon Oil. It can mean a new move to nonunion firms.

When one starts providing those kinds of examples, one
suddenly realizes that one person's entrepreneurship is another's
poison. The point is not that this is the only way to think about the
possible consequences of entrepreneurship but to remind us that we
do need to think hard about what it means and what consequences it
has. I hope our discussions today will help us do that. Entrepreneurship per se does not give us much of a guide to many of the key yet
strategic decisions that corporations have to make.

One can also distinguish between entrepreneurship in the
classic sense that Schumpeter used the term and what is coming to
be known as intrapreneurship — the latter defined as the process of
introducing innovations within the firm. We will be talking about
both this afternoon. Intrapreneurship is more consistent with classic
notions about the benefits of decentralization. It is not limited to
high-level managers. Indeed, it is consistent with the recent focus on
business teams and with providing an opportunity for even
blue-collar workers to have their ideas for change listened to and
accepted.

All this is to say that I look forward to our conversations
with great interest. I think it will be a valuable exercise for all of us.

Stimulating and Managing Corporate Entrepreneurship: The Auto Industry Connection

Rosabeth Moss Kanter

To an observer, this is a time of enormous, almost revolutionary, change in an industry that was until recently thought to be in deep trouble and incapable of change unless forced down its throat from the outside.

Consider the implications of these U.S. examples for the structure of the industry, with reverberations throughout the entire chain from materials suppliers through retail dealers:

General Motors has just announced its new venture start-up, the Saturn Project, a separate subsidiary developing its own business systems, work processes (such as modular assembly), and dealer network — without being subject to current GM policies and procedures.

General Motors also appears to be actively pursuing new business development opportunities in partnership with other organizations. With the acquisition of Electronic Data Systems, the New United Motor Manufacturing joint venture with Toyota, and rumored nonauto acquisitions, the company is in a position to use knowledge gained from these partnerships to benefit its core business as well as to seek synergies between automotive and nonautomotive enterprises that permit new business development. Entrepreneurial spinoffs (such as selling internal information processing or telecommunications

3

capacity outside) may result. At minimum, the new partnerships are opening the doors to changing GM's corporate culture—toward their partners' model (Holusha 1985; Darlin and Guiles 1984).

Technological innovations provide other opportunities for synergistic business development, both to improve existing components and to be exploited as commercial ventures in their own right. For example, Magnequench, a new class of high performance permanent magnets invented by GM research scientists, is used on a Delco Remy cranking motor and can also be sold, generating multiple paybacks from R&D investments. There are similar examples in Ford's plastics division.

New service businesses offering in-house technology for external use are resulting in profitable small spin-off ventures within the large manufacturing companies. One truck company has established a wholly owned subsidiary to provide an array of in-house, computer-aided services to the end users of its products. The venture is a second generation spinoff of an even earlier initiative providing leasing support to its dealer network.

Chrysler introduced a new category of vehicle in 1983, the minivan—not a truck but a personal-use utility vehicle. The competition soon followed suit. The opportunity to create not only new products but also new automotive *categories* is one sign of industry revitalization.

Throughout the industry, the number of separate parts suppliers to the major manufacturers is being reduced, and closer working relationships established, including use of such widely praised methods as just-in-time inventory. (Indeed, new Justice Department guidelines on "vertical accords," announced in the *New York Times* in January 1985, are easing the way to more integration between suppliers and manufacturers.)

The dealer franchise system, which largely took its present form in the period following World War II (see Macauley 1966), may be poised for major change. Easing the way for single ownership of multiple dealerships could professionalize dealership management as well as lead to more auto "superdealers" or to new retail combinations. Ford's suburban shopping-mall displays are among new marketing techniques being explored. (In recent years, dealers themselves have needed to become more entrepreneurial, using their service units, for example, as profit centers, new customer lures, and sources of competitive sales advantage.)

And, of course, developments in manufacturing technology, the use of semiconductors, and joint labor-management improvement projects all continue to affect the cost structure of the industry, while internationalization of markets portends changes in product design, parts sourcing, and manufacturing location. New entrants to the U.S. market from Yugoslavia and Korea provide additional evidence that the industry may be "de-maturing" (Abernathy, Kantrow, and Clark 1983). And changes in technology permitting manufacturing flexibility that can enable profitability at lower volumes may encourage still other new entrants.

As the auto industry restructures, new concepts are being explored in a number of domains beyond product innovation. Sourcing and distribution are being rethought; business development is being viewed more broadly as involving commercial possibilities beyond the core product; and new forms of partnership are emerging, from joint ventures through closer supplier relationships through labor-management cooperation. Recent research by Robert Reich, for example, shows that the number of U.S.-Japan joint ventures has doubled between 1980 and 1984.

Is change possible? Do opportunities exist for growth and expansion? Those are metaphysical questions. They cannot be answered in the absence of trying. If no one tries, we do not have a fair test.

Better questions for older industries are not whether change is possible but *whether it is likely*, not whether opportunities exist but *whether anyone will act on them*. Research by Donald Schon (1967), among others, indicates that most innovation in traditional industries originates outside the industry—demonstrating that (a) change is possible; and (b) if all else remains the same, it is less likely to come from current players. So, we need to focus our attention not on the industry but on the organizations participating in it, readying them to encourage more entrepreneurial behavior.

I am making four assumptions about innovation and the entrepreneurial process that drives it, derived from detailed research on 10 companies and a briefer review of almost 80 others for *The Change Masters*, as well as contact with nearly 100 major companies since the book was published.

Proposition 1: Major barriers to innovation and entrepreneurship lie at the organization level rather than at the industry level. Perhaps the single biggest barrier is an ineffable human one: lack of imagination—inability to conceive of anything different. This, in turn, is created or reinforced by organizational rigidities making it hard to see, develop, or act on new ideas and by a series of fixed assumptions about the value of repeating, with only minor modifications, past behavior. To increase entrepreneurship in a so-called "mature" industry, then, requires new organizational structures and management methods.

Proposition 2: Behind big innovations or major venture developments is a series of smaller-scale innovations supporting them. In order to make a big new idea work, many other changes in surrounding systems or practices are also required. To emphasize only technology, for example, or only product features, is not enough because many other innovations may be necessary to get the product manufactured or distributed or product parts sourced or purchases financed. It thus defeats entrepreneurship to focus only one part of an organization on innovation—e.g., R&D—while rewarding the rest for preserving the status quo. An entrepreneurial organization is capable of innovating in every aspect of its operations.

Proposition 3: Concomitantly, once an organization embarks on a course requiring more innovation, more new ventures and new products, it is impossible to fully determine and direct this process solely from the top. To be successful, more entrepreneurship (in the form of creativity, tinkering, and experimentation) will be required at middle and lower levels, and more "spontaneous" innovation will need to emanate from the ranks. Top-driven and spontaneous innovation are mutually supportive. *Both* are necessary.

Proposition 4: The style of management and organization needed for innovation and entrepreneurship is different from that suited to the efficient repetition of the past in ongoing operations where change is not as necessary. Organizations clearly need some of both (Lawrence and Dyer 1983). The problem is when one style completely dominates, thereby cutting off either innovation or efficiency. The trick lies in designing the organization to permit opportunities for both – of course, in appropriate proportion given the tasks of a work unit.

I will first briefly define the multiple domains for innovation involved in successful entrepreneurship, then show *why* the special requirements of managing successful innovation are hard to meet when administrative, "command"-oriented management interferes with the logic of the entrepreneurial process. I will then outline the features of high-innovation organizations managed by the more entrepreneurial mode of "mutual adjustment" and describe some of the tactics American companies are using to stimulate more innovation and entrepreneurship, both within their own "borders" and in partnership with other organizations through joint ventures and closer working relationships.

Multiple Innovations behind
Entrepreneurial Successes

Many of today's current success stories, in which new entrants to established industries have gained significant market shares, involve not only an imaginative new concept (or a previously ignored concept that fills a neglected niche in the market – a reason many give for the success of Japanese cars in the U.S. market in the 1970s) but also a large number of new organizational practices that support the central business concept and make it possible.

> *USA Today*, for example, was a new national newspaper founded at a time when local newspapers were in financial difficulty (many of them merging or folding) and when competition from nonprint media were said to make newspapers a declining factor in the market. *USA Today* was able to gain a foothold and grow because of a number of innovations supporting its core innovative concept. Some involved product features, such as the use of color and graphics to give the product a new and appealing look. Others involved the application of new technology to print a paper nationwide, such as extensive use of satellite transmission of information.

Still other innovations involved distribution techniques that made the product easily accessible to
prime customers: the use of street-corner vending
boxes in key locations and distributing copies at
airports, in airline clubs, and on planes.

People Express, a successful new airline, benefited
from deregulation certainly—but it also entered a
troubled industry. Its low-cost, no-frills service not
only filled a market niche but also, its founder claims,
increased the total market. Its ability to offer
lower-cost travel, at an impressive profit and without
the cooperation of other airlines for interline
agreements, was a function, in turn, of other
innovations. It established its headquarters and a
new hub at Newark's virtually abandoned North
Terminal. But it is the company's innovations in
human resource management that have given People
Express the lowest cost per mile of any major airline.

All employees are also owners, holding about
$40,000 worth of stock on the average. They are all
cross-trained and cross-utilized—pilots serving as
accountants when not flying, flight attendants as
reservations agents. Even top management spends a
mandatory day as part of the on-board crew, to keep
them in touch with customers. And a high level of
teamwork, in virtually self-managed teams, reduces
the need for supervisory personnel. Labor
productivity is high, then, because of a combination of
practices that boost employees' commitment and
stake in airline profitability and that use them well
and flexibly.

I am not suggesting that newspapers and airlines are fully
comparable to the auto industry. But these kinds of examples
hopefully make clear that behind entrepreneurship in the
macrosense—new business development or new venture creation
—we often find many innovations in every system that makes up the
company. For example, the success of Honda in selling motorcycles
in the U.S. was a function not only of new technology and attractive

product features but also of developing a new image for the product by finding new distribution channels.

Entrepreneurship thus consists of more than simply offering a new product; it may involve sourcing its materials in new ways, making it in new ways, organizing the human resources attached to it in new ways, distributing it in new ways, and servicing it in new ways. And it involves doing these things in an atmosphere of uncertainty — without the certainty that tried-and-true methods for tried-and-true products brings. But entrepreneurs dare to innovate, despite the uncertainty, and they are willing to innovate in every aspect of operations.

Some analysts have pointed to the high risks in innovation in the auto industry. As Lawrence White (1982) summarized it:

> New models require four to five years of lead time. Hundreds of millions of dollars must be spent long before a new model is introduced. Buyers are clearly fickle and, because demand is largely for replacement, can delay purchases and retain their existing cars longer. Swings of 15% or more in annual industry sales are not uncommon, and even larger swings in individual company sales are quite possible. The implications of this industry structure for innovation are profound. The high barriers to entry mean that if an independent innovator has a 'better idea' for a vehicle, a major component (e.g., engine or transmission), or a manufacturing process, his only hope for eventual success lies in convincing one among a literal handful of manufacturers of that innovation's worth. He has virtually no hope of establishing himself in the motor vehicle industry so as to produce the innovation himself. . . . Further, product change is necessary to attract the replacement demand. But product change is risky, and the more fundamental the change, the riskier it is.

So White concludes that gradualism is likely to be the favored innovation strategy.

While views such as this reflect historical experience and would locate problems of entrepreneurship in industry conditions, it may be a limited view. This is made clear by looking at the success and failure of new corporate ventures where the problems are clearly organizational.

Among the most important reasons for the failure of new ventures in established corporations is an attempt to "force-fit" the venture into an inappropriate corporate mold. The new venture is managed through an invariant set of practices that might work well for ongoing products but that tend to reduce the venture's chances for success by failing to take account of its new and different requirements. In one unfortunate example, a large manufacturer of controls that were sold through contractors developed a promising new product that could go right to consumers. Because the company assigned its manufacture to an existing division using technology designed for other purposes, costs were too high to make the retail price attractive, and the existing marketing staff had no experience with consumer sales. Yet competitors had excellent success with an almost identical product. Only in retrospect, in a session I held with top management critiquing the venture failures, did these issues become clear.

In short, corporate entrepreneurship frequently fails because organizational rigidities prevent its success, not always because the concept was a poor one.

Among the factors limiting innovation are assumptions about the conditions for business success — assumptions that may indeed be borne out by immediate financial returns but are still largely taken on faith in the absence of the testing of alternative strategies. Company strategists may assume that consumers like what they have, though in case after case entrepreneurs make a market where one never existed and would not have been discovered by market testing — as Apple's phenomenal success in personal computers makes clear.

Some observers of the U.S. motor vehicle industry have concluded that product and process innovation has played only a limited role in the industry from the period following World War II through the 1970s, and, furthermore, that the dominant impetus for the innovations that have occurred came from outside the major manufacturing companies — either from parts suppliers or from federal regulations. Industry insiders naturally take a different view and point to large R&D expenditures, but Lawrence White (1982) cites a long list of technological developments in which suppliers played major roles: from power steering through aluminum engines and tinted glass. (I should note that even this argument, ironically, revolves around a set of limited assumptions about what constitutes the *realm for innovation* — only new technology or product features, and not other business systems and practices.)

At the same time, some of the noteworthy changes that have taken place in automobile manufacturing companies over the past decade involve new management practices and organizational arrangements that support innovation by creating more flexibility, particularly in terms of shop-floor problem solving, the application of new manufacturing or information technology, and streamlined inventory-management techniques.

Now, as manufacturers are beginning to rethink supplier relationships and distribution systems and to develop new concepts like the Saturn that will, apparently, be able to "invent" its own internal systems and dealer arrangements, it is an appropriate time to consider the kind of management and organization necessary for taking a more entrepreneurial stance in *every* area of the business. This will also help us see what might stand in the way — the legacy of traditional practices that can hold innovation back.

Recall that the term "entrepreneurship" means the creation of new combinations. *At its very root, the entrepreneurial process of innovation and change is at odds with the administrative process of ensuring repetitions of the past.* The management of innovation and change requires a different set of practices and different modes of organization than the management of ongoing, established operations where the desire for or expectation of change is minimal. Howard Stevenson and David Gumpert (1985) have cast this management difference in terms of the contrast between the "promoter"-type stance of the entrepreneur, driven by perception of opportunity, and the "trustee"-like stance of the administrator, driven to conserve resources already controlled.

In organizations in which innovation and entrepreneurship have been only minor themes in business strategy, and in which the risks associated with major change have led to cautious or gradualist stances, we are likely to find an accumulation of policies and practices that make major innovation difficult — entrepreneurial management prevented by the demands of administrative management.

What Is Different about Entrepreneurial Management

The creation and exploitation of new products, new processes, or new systems has four special requirements and unique situations to manage because of characteristics of the innovation process itself. Understanding the requirements of innovation makes clear why entrepreneurship needs to be managed differently from ongoing operations.

Uncertainty

The innovation process involves little or no precedent or experience base to use to make forecasts about results. Hoped-for timetables may prove unrealistic. Anticipated costs may be overrun. Results are highly uncertain. This situation thus requires:

> committed visionary leadership willing to initiate and sustain effort on the basis of faith in the idea;

> the existence of "patient money," or capital that does not have to show a short-term return; and

> a great deal of planning flexibility, to adjust the original concept to the emerging realities.

But these requirements can run counter to those aspects of administrative management that may require instead:

> Detailed management in advance of resource commitments (e.g., in one company the list of the *analyses* to be done itself runs ten pages).

> Fairly rapid returns on investment or a very high probable revenue base from the activity (e.g., packaged goods companies uninterested in under $100 million/year). (Dean [1974] describes the "mismatch" between the pace of innovation and management's time horizons.)

> High-level sign-off on a "plan" and agreement to a set of procedures or steps, with the expectation that they be followed without deviation—measuring managers on adherence to plan rather than on results.

Knowledge Intensivity

The innovation process is knowledge intensive, relying on individual human intelligence and creativity. New experiences are accumulated at a fast pace; the learning curve is steep. The knowledge that resides in the participants in the innovation effort is not always codified or codifiable for transfer to others. Efforts are very vulnerable to turnover, because of the loss of this knowledge and experience. This situation thus requires:

> stability among the participants involved in an innovation effort, especially the venture manager or visionary leader;

> a high degree of commitment among all participants, as well as close, team-oriented working relationships with high mutual respect, to encourage rapid and effective exchange of knowledge among participants; and

> intense and concentrated effort focused inward on the project.

But these requirements may run counter to those aspects of administrative management that instead allow:

> regular turnover of managers because of a lock-step career system that ties rewards to promotions and thus requires job changes;

> bureaucratic assignment of managers or personnel without regard to their degree of belief in the effort or their compatibility with each other; and

> reporting requirements that disrupt activities and distract participants by asking them to prepare special analyses for upper management or attend meetings unrelated to advancing the work of the innovation team.

Competition with Alternatives

In the innovation process, there is always competition with alternative courses of action. (The pursuit of the air-cooled engine at Honda Motor, for example, drew time and resources away from improving the water-cooled engine [Sakiya 1982].) Furthermore, sometimes the very existence of a potential innovation poses a threat to vested interests — whether the interest is that of a salesperson receiving high commissions on current products or of the advocates of a competing direction. Indeed, observers point to "political" problems as one of the major causes for the failure of corporate entrepreneurship (Fast 1976). This situation thus requires:

champions or sponsors who will argue for the course of action, who will sustain the vision;

coalitions of backers or supporters from a number of areas willing to lend credence (and resources) to the project;

sufficient job security throughout the organization that innovations are not seen as position-threatening; and

identification with the success of the whole organization.

But these requirements may be difficult to meet if managers have been selected, trained, promoted, and rewarded in an administrative mode that encourages instead:

cautious, conservative stands that involve betting on sure things only (e.g., in one company requiring risk analyses, a preference for no-risk new products);

interdepartmental rivalry and competition for scarce resources or rewards, with each area having to "defeat" others to ensure its continuing existence, and rewards based only on individual unit performance; and

lack of confrontation or constructive arguing out of differences, but resorting to underground sabotage instead.

"Boundary" Crossing

The innovation process is rarely if ever contained solely within one unit. First, there is evidence that many of the best ideas are interdisciplinary or interfunctional in origin—as connoted by the root meaning of entrepreneurship as the development of "new combinations"—or benefit from broader perspectives and information from outside of the area primarily responsible for the innovation. Second, regardless of the origin of innovations, they inevitably send out ripples and reverberations to other organizational units, whose behavior may be required to change in light of the needs of innovations, or whose cooperation is necessary if an innovation is to be fully developed or exploited. Or there may be the need to generate unexpected innovations in another domain in order to support the primary product, like the need to design a new motor to make the first Apple computer viable. This situation thus requires:

> Enlarging the focus of participants in the innovation process to take account of the perspectives of other units or disciplines. (What I call "kaleidoscope" thinking is at the heart of the creative process in innovation—the use of new angles or perspectives to reshuffle the parts to make a new pattern, thus challenging conventional assumptions.)

> Early involvement of functions or units that may play a role at some later stage of the venture or innovation effort.

> A high degree of commitment by functions or players outside of the innovation-producing unit to the innovation.

> A high degree of interaction across functions or units—and thus more interunit teamwork.

> Reciprocal influence among functions.

But these requirements can run counter to the typical administrative-bureaucratic pattern that instead fosters:

narrowing of focus via an emphasis on specialization,
single-discipline careers, and limited communication
among functions or disciplines;

a preference for homogeneity over diversity, for
orthodoxy over new perspectives;

measurement of functions or units (or divisions) on
their own performance alone, so that rewards drive
behavior that maximizes unit-specific returns rather
than partnership contributions to the projects of other
units; and

structural arrangements and reporting systems that
separate (segment) functions or units and assign each
a set of steps in a process assumed to be linear rather
than reciprocal and interactional.

Overall, then, it is not surprising that research on the problems of
new corporate ventures tends to attribute failures to such common
factors as the requirement for inappropriate planning/analysis and
the pressure for faster results; turnover on the venture team and
lack of committed leadership; the politics of gaining sponsorship or
championing within the corporation (or the perils of getting the
"wrong" sponsorship); and interfunctional conflicts that either slow
the process down or steer the project in an inappropriate direction
(von Hippel 1977; Block 1982, 1983; Hobson and Morrison 1983;
Fast 1976; MacMillan, Block, and Narasimha 1984).

Note that the emphasis in entrepreneurial management is
on *commitment*, not *consensus*. The entrepreneurial process can be
driven by single-minded fanatics who convice a few others that their
vision is worth pursuing, but complete consensus throughout the
organization is not necessary—in the development phase—as long as
the innovation team itself is committed (although it may be necessary to diffuse the innovation once developed). Indeed, it is the
search for total consensus on every action through a company that
promotes homogeneity and orthodoxy. The desire for the safety of
noncontroversial decisions confines activities to the least
controversial or least threatening to status quo interests. But the
entrepreneurial process, in contrast, permits diversity and allows
conflict to surface, while encouraging temporary coalitions of the
committed to form and operate.

From Command to Mutual Adjustment

Administrative management works to hold things in place, preventing deviation from established practice, once rules are made. It is compatible with a "command" system in which every person and every function knows its place. When this type of management results in high degrees of compartmentalization of responsibilities and limited contact between a large number of differentiated statuses (distinctions of level, of function, of units), I have referred to it as *"segmentalism"* — an approach to organizing and managing that discourages change, even in the face of obvious problems with the status quo (Kanter 1983).

But the entrepreneurial process requires instead more reliance on the particular persons involved, closer working relationships, the ability to depart from tradition, and a governance system that is one of continual negotiation and mutual adjustment among all participants with something to contribute to the effort. This approach to organizing can be called *"integrative"* — an emphasis on bringing together rather than separating activities or people — and the governance system called a partnership or *mutual adjustment* model.

A simple proposition in organizational theory holds that under conditions of low uncertainty and high predictability about both inputs and outcomes, it is effective to manage by rules, paperwork, and other impersonal means administered through clearly established centers of command that issue orders. But under conditions of high uncertainty and low predictability, it is more effective to manage by personal communication and negotiation — in part because of the sheer inability to issue enough commands to cover every contingency.

Thus, entrepreneurship requires a system of management by mutual adjustment instead of a system of management by command. Management by mutual adjustment, in turn, relies on integrative organizational conditions: a close working relationship among all participants and mutual respect fostered by the absence of status differences, overlapping responsibilities, and concern for joint goals. It is partnership-oriented and allows for temporary alliances among equals instead of submersion of parties in a hierarchy — e.g., joint ventures versus acquisitions, borrowing or renting assets rather than owning them.

All established organizations clearly need both systems. They need a *command* system for those areas where repeating the past is necessary, where predictable products or services are to be turned out reliably and uniformly according to an established blueprint, and where efficiencies are to be gained through a learning curve derived from numerous repetitions. And they need a *mutual adjustment* system wherever innovation is desired, problems need to be solved, and new techniques or methods are sought.

Maximizing *both* efficiency and innovation is required for an organization to be adaptive (Lawrence and Dyer 1983). Even in a fairly new company developing new products in a growing market, both systems play a role. Mitchell Kapor, the 34-year-old founder and CEO of Lotus Development Corporation, a highly successful software firm, acknowledged this need for two simultaneous management systems:

> To be a successful enterprise, we have to do two apparently contradictory things quite well: we have to stay innovative and creative, but at the same time we have to be tightly controlled about certain aspects of our corporate behavior. But I think that what you have to do about paradox is embrace it. So we have the kind of company where certain things are very loose and other things are very tight. The whole art of management is sorting things into the loose pile or the tight pile and then watching them carefully. (Boston *Globe*, 27 January 1985)

Organizations where administrative command systems dominate sometimes establish a separate system for entrepreneurship and innovation, running, in effect, two organizations side-by-side. One example is the "parallel organization" concept at use in the QWL program at General Motors and other companies — a second, participative organization of temporary task forces added to the operating organization with its clear specification of roles and responsibilities and its numerous distinctions between functions and levels (Stein and Kanter 1980). Another example is the establishment of new venture units in large corporations, units that operate by different principles than the organization running established businesses, like the separate organization that developed the IBM PC or GM's Saturn subsidiary.

Though every company, depending on the tasks at hand, needs some mix of command and mutual adjustment systems, the ability to innovate requires a shift towards the mutual adjustment mode. Companies that are successful in industries where innovation is essential tend to be dominated by the integrative principle of management by mutual adjustment more than by the segmentalist principle of management by command. This permits them to behave entrepreneurially in every domain, and to take advantage of "spontaneous" as well as officially mandated innovations.

Stimulating Innovation and Supporting Entrepreneurship: Characteristics of High Innovation Companies

Innovation and new venture development may originate as a deliberate and official decision of the highest levels of management, or they may be the more or less "spontaneous" creation of mid-level people who take the initiative to solve a problem in new ways or to develop a proposal for change. Of course, highly successful companies allow both, and even official top management decisions to undertake a development effort benefit from the "spontaneous" creativity of those below. But regardless of origin, for the idea to be turned into living reality capable of generating financial returns, certain organizational characteristics are generally present. Those companies with high levels of enterprise tend to have these conditions reflected more widely in their on-going practices (Kanter 1983).

The Facilitating Conditions: Jobs, Structure, Culture, and "Power Tools"

Jobs

Innovation is aided when jobs are defined broadly rather than narrowly, when people have a range of skills to use and tasks to perform to give them a "feel" for the organization, and when assignments focus on results to be achieved rather than rules or procedures to be followed. This, in turn, gives people the mandate to solve problems, to respond creatively to new conditions, to note changed requirements around them, or to improve practices—rather than mindlessly following procedures derived from the past. Furthermore, when broader definitions of jobs permit task domains to overlap rather than divide cleanly, people are encouraged to gain the perspective of others with whom they must now interact and, therefore, take more responsibility for the total task rather than simply their own small piece of it. This leads to the broader perspectives that help stimulate innovation.

In areas that benefit from more enterprise and problem solving on the part of jobholders, bigger jobs work better. This is the principle behind work systems that give employees responsibility for a major piece of a production process and allow them to make decisions about how and when to divide up the tasks. Pay-for-skill systems similarly encourage broader perspectives by rewarding people for learning more jobs.

A proliferation of job classifications and fine distinctions between steps in what are really connected processes (e.g., the distinction between many types of engineers specializing in only one step in a conceive-to-design-to-build process) has inhibited innovation in many large, segmentalist American companies. Individual jobholders need take no responsibility for ultimate outcomes as long as they perform their own narrow task adequately. Where jobs are narrowly and rigidly defined, people have little incentive to engage in either "spontaneous" innovation (self-generated problem-solving attempts with those in neighboring tasks) or to join together across job categories for larger top-directed innovation efforts—especially if differences in job classification also confer differential status or privilege. Companies even lose basic efficiency as some tasks remain undone while waiting for the person with the "right" job classification to become available—even though others in another classification may have the skills and the time. And people tend to actively avoid doing any more work than the minimum, falling back on the familiar excuse, "That's not *my* job"—a refrain whose frequent repetition is a good sign of a troubled company.

But examples of high levels of entrepreneurial effort make clear this effort between job definitions and the enterprise necessary for innovation:

> In some high-tech computer companies, people in professional and managerial jobs are regularly exhorted to "invent" their own jobs or are given broad trouble-shooting assignments to "fix it" by "doing the right thing." Organization charts can be produced on demand, but by the time people add all the exceptions, the dotted lines reflecting multiple responsibilities and the circles around special teams or task forces, the whole thing resembles a "plate of spaghetti," as one observer put it, more than a chain

of command and a division of labor. While this situation can also appear chaotic and undisciplined, it does result in more people assuming responsibility to solve problems and make improvements — and as my middle manager research for *The Change Masters* showed, high levels of innovation in every function.

A major manufacturer of household products can cite numerous instances of spontaneous problem-solving effort by employees who are part of self-managed "business teams" responsible for producing their product in their part of the factory without supervision. Over the last ten years, work teams have gradually taken responsibility for every function in the factory, and they conceive of themselves as "owning" and managing their own small business.

To capture such benefits, New United Motor Manufacturing, the GM-Toyota joint venture in Fremont, California, has enlarged production jobs. Teams of five to twelve workers, guided by a team leader, get broad responsibility and divide up the specific tasks themselves; each worker is theoretically able to do any job. In contrast to the dozens of job classifications that existed when the plant was run by GM, there is just one classification for production workers and three for skilled trades.

Organizational Structure

When it comes to innovation, "small is beautiful," and flexible is even better. Or at least small is beautiful as long as the small unit includes a connection with every function or discipline necessary to create the final product, as well as the autonomy to go ahead and do it.

In order to get the kind of interfunctional or interdisciplinary integration that innovation requires, close relationships are demanded — working teams or venture teams that are functionally complete, on which every necessary function is represented.

This is why the idea of dividing into smaller but complete business units is so appealing to organizations seeking continual innovation. All the players are right there, to be linked closely in the innovation process. (And for all their cumbersomeness in practice, "matrix" reporting relationships acknowledging multiple responsibilities keep interfunctional links alive.) In smaller business units it is possible to maintain much closer working relationships across functions than in larger ones—one of the reasons for Hewlett-Packard's classic growth strategy of dividing divisions into two when they reached more than 2,000 people or $100,000,000 in sales.

Even where economies of scale push for larger units, the cross-functional project or product team within a single facility (captured in such ideas as the factory within a factory) helps keep the communication and the connection alive. Or the "skunkworks" of creative innovators given their own charter and territory speeds the development process.

Finally, it is important that those with local knowledge have the ability to experiment using that knowledge—within whatever guidelines or limits get set at higher levels. Innovation is discouraged when those with the responsibilty lack the authority to make those changes that they feel will benefit their business.

Culture

High innovation organizations have in common the high value they place on people and their potential—what I have come to call a "culture of pride" that expects and rewards high levels of achievement and assumes that investments in people pay off. A mutual adjustment system of management, in contrast to a command system, requires a high degree of respect for people—not only on the part of the company but also on the part of all of the players who must back and support each other's ideas. The investment in people that characterizes high innovation settings is slightly different from the more paternalistic principle of lifetime employment. While many high innovation companies try to maintain lifetime employment policies, which certainly offer security in exchange for loyalty, this by itself is not responsible for the level of enterprise found in them. Instead, it is the expectation of continuing growth of contribution over time that fosters more entrepreneurial stances. This is reflected in large dollar amounts spent on training and development—and in the emphasis on having the best human resource systems in general.

Operationally, a "culture of pride" is fostered through abundant praise and recognition—a proliferation of awards and recognition mechanisms that continuously hold up the standards for display and publicly acknowledge the people who meet and exceed them. High innovation settings are marked by their celebrations and award ceremonies, trophies and wall plaques, and merit badges and awards ("local hero" awards and "extra mile" awards and "atta-boys") that visibly communicate respect for people and their abilities to contribute. Merit reward systems (as opposed to automatic cost-of-living adjustments but little or no merit component) also convey the company's recognition of performance.

Low innovation settings, by contrast, seem begrudging about praise, operate in ways that signal that all important knowledge comes from outside the company, and expect people's recognition for achievement to be the fact that they have kept their job. I have even found a company that gives significant monetary awards for above-and-beyond contributions — but keeps these all secret.

The Tools to Move into Action

The entrepreneurial process requires three kinds of "power tools" to move ideas into action — information, support (backing or legitimacy, appropriate sponsorship or championing), and resources. Of course, when large projects are initiated at the top of the organization and handed a staff and a checkbook, there is little issue about acquiring the tools to accomplish innovation — although even in this case, managers can run across problems of access to the tools they need. But for instances of spontaneous entrepreneurship, generated within the organization and still lacking the status of a major and official project, access to "power tools" can be critical in whether bold new initiatives are ever seeded. Access to power tools is easier in high innovation settings because of organizational structure and practice.

Information is more readily available in high innovation settings because of open communication patterns that make data accessible throughout the organization. For example, operating data may be shared down to the shop floor, or face-to-face communication may be emphasized, or norms may bar "closed meetings" — all common practices in some high-technology companies.

Support or collaboration is encouraged in high innovation settings by the dense networks of ties that connect people across diverse areas of the company, because of cross-discipline career paths, membership on task forces and cross-area teams, frequent conferences or meetings across areas, or even whole-unit parties like Silicon Valley's Friday beer busts. Easy access to potential sponsors or champions is also more likely where title consciousness is minimal, and the chain of command is not a pecking order.

Resources are easier to get in high innovation settings because they are decentralized and loosely controlled. That is, more people have budgetary authority and can make commitments for "seed capital" for new activities. Or there are more sources of slack—uncommitted funds—that can be allocated to innovation. There is discretionary time and discretionary resources that can be managed flexibly, used for experimentation, or reinvested in new approaches.

Rules for Stifling Innovation

Because the conditions for entrepreneurship are so often missing in many large corporations, I have proposed (tongue in cheek) that many of them operate as though guided by a set of principles for preventing innovation and entrepreneurship. These are some of the "rules" that would form part of such a "how not to do it" guide:

1. Be suspicious of new ideas from below—because they're new and because they're from below. After all, if the idea were any good, the people at the top would have thought of it already.

2. Insist that people who need approval to act go through many other levels of the organization first. (That makes it easy to avoid saying no, as most people will be killed off at other levels—and anyway, the process will be slowed down so much that most decision makers are likely to be in a different job by then.)

3. Express criticism freely, withhold praise, and instill job insecurity—because it keeps people on their toes and shows the company has standards. (It is part of the old "macho" school of management practiced by executives like Harold Geneen that seemed to hold that people did their best work when terrified.)

4. Be control conscious. Count everything that can be counted — and as often as possible. (When there are many, many measures, the company guarantees that all behavior goes just to the measures — people will be unlikely to depart from the strict rules of performance. And this also guards against innnovation by ensuring that there is no "slack" — no spare time or dollars or paper clips — that can be used to tinker or experiment or conceive of doing anything differently than it is done today.)

5. Never forget that the people at the top already know everything important there is to know about this business. (Kanter 1983: 101)

Unwritten — but certainly not unnoticed — "rules" such as these pervade corporations characterized by a command system of management and a segmentalist structure. And in trying to live by these rules, people steer away from the riskier — but sometimes more rewarding — business of innovation. It is these rules of management behavior-in-practice, even more than pronouncements built into corporate strategy, that account for whether an entrepreneurial spirit pervades a company.

Special Programs for Encouraging Corporate Entrepreneurship

In addition to developing a structure and culture conducive to innovation and entrepreneurship, many companies are beginning to institute deliberate programs to encourage it.

1.   Making sure that current systems, structures, and practices do not present insurmountable roadblocks to the flexibility and fast action needed for innovation.

Reducing unnecessary "bureaucracy." For example, a major petroleum company has made a number of significant changes in order to remove roadblocks to entrepreneurship. Its exploration area reduced the number of approvals necessary for land acquisition, finding that each additional approval was associated with a 15 percent loss of productivity. Another division conducted a "hog law" review, soliciting views from employees about no-longer-necessary

rules and regulations that were impeding change. Still another
department reorganized to remove levels of hierarchy, after
concluding that the additional levels did not "add value" to activities
but simply slowed them down.

   Changing internal budgeting and accounting procedures. One
large household-products manufacturer has discovered that its internal financial systems may discourage investment in new technologies
because all expenditures must be justified in terms of immediate cost
savings. A leading bank decided to separate budgets for ongoing
products and activities from investments in new ones for just this
reason, and they have started noting levels of investments
expenditure as a positive step in department reviews as well as, in
the aggregate, in their annual report. The bank has also begun to
encourage the divestment of old or less-profitable products and techniques in favor of new ones by allowing departments to retain most
of any cost savings they produce for investment in new products and
developments.

   *Reducing "segmentalism" and encouraging integration across
departments and functions.* Actions that improve communication and
information flow across units and levels are one step. Some
companies with a legacy of excessive segmentation of activities are
restructuring to create more business-specific, customer-specific, or
product-specific teams across functions. Others are stressing
interdepartmental improvement projects or idea exchanges. They
are trying to ease the flow of information, support, and resources
across areas – the key "power tools."

2.   *Providing the incentives and tools for entrepreneurial projects.*

   Internal "venture capital" and special project budgets.
Following the lead of 3M, and now several other major organizations
such as Eastman Kodak, an increasing number of companies are
setting up special "innovation banks" to fund new ventures or
innovations outside of operating budgets. General Motors set up
such a fund with the UAW in the 1984 labor agreement to seek new
ventures that could preserve jobs, in light of job-reductions, with new
technology. Through such special "banks," large new ventures can
be supported inside the company as a separate business. But
perhaps more significantly, many small development activities can
be undertaken that would otherwise find no place in a line manager's
budget (because of the typical requirement for immediate cost
savings or ROI for expenditures).

Thus, efforts that are more experimental, may take more time to bring returns, or do not fit neatly within existing areas can still find a home. This is useful not only for those innovations in products or technology that might normally fall within the scope of an R&D operation, but also for numerous other special projects in marketing or information systems or personnel or dealer relations that can themselves net considerable payoffs. A large computer manufacturer has funded innovative organizational improvement projects out of a corporate innovation council.

Discretionary funds and discretionary time. Simply leaving a portion of budgets uncommitted, to be used as managers see fit, can stimulate innovation. Similarly with time. 3M is again the most noteworthy model because of their formalization of the 15 percent rule—that up to 15 percent of employees' time may be spent on projects of their own choosing.

A "dry hole" or "portfolio" approach to innovation. Top management can and should act as sponsors of innovation, devoting more of their time to new venture creation and innovation in internal systems and techniques than to the control of ongoing activities. A portfolio approach means seeding many diverse projects and many diverse experiments—smaller scale and at lower funding levels than the few traditional projects in most large companies—with an expectation that some will fail, but some will pay off. The "dry hole" analogy is from oil exploration, where a large number of holes are drilled with the knowledge that only a small portion will produce yields. But the more holes that are drilled—and the increasing intelligence brought to each by learning from "failures"—the greater likelihood of major results.

Of course, there is a balancing factor: the importance of good aim, of efforts focused in areas likely to pay off. Increased experimentation does not necessitate acting on *every* idea. Long range plans and management priority setting can help focus local initiative so that more "drilled holes" produce yields.

Performance review and compensation geared to innovation. While many companies engage in the rhetoric of innovation, their methods of appraising and rewarding people may still be tied to short-term revenues and profits, which discourages innovation. For this reason, companies are increasingly including the development of creative new activities as part of MBO's and performance appraisals and making it harder for people to "do well" if they are simply continuing the tried and true. And they are also considering much larger rewards for successful innovation, from phantom stock to a percent of the return from a new venture, in exchange for deferral of reward (other than basic salary) that can accompany longer-term projects or ventures.

Indeed, the entire topic of compensation will be rethought in the decade ahead and will itself be the target of innovation, as a more "entrepreneurial" era brings with it a growth of vehicles tying compensation to company financial performance through everything from ownershiplike devices such as gainsharing to actual employee ownership. Finally, some companies are also experimenting with ways to reward and recognize the sponsors and champions of innovators, not just the doers, to encourage more high-level support for innovation.

3.   Seeking synergies across business areas, so that new opportunities are discovered in new combinations at the same time that business units retain operating autonomy.

Joint projects and ventures — intercompany, interdivisional, company-with-supplier, company with vendor, etc. Joint ventures, requiring a partnership stance and governance by mutual adjustment, are increasingly common as companies discover the synergies that come from combining resources for specific purposes rather than acquiring a whole company — a route for new venture development that innovation experts such as Edward Roberts (1980) have been encouraging. (Howard Stevenson and David Gumpert [1985] point out that "trustees" feel they must "own" all resources themselves in order to better control them, whereas entrepreneurs are willing to "rent" them, find them through joint ventures, or turn to subcontractors.) Even joint ventures across divisions of a single company provide promising avenues for business development. But often, traditional practices have discouraged this, often by the ways in which the performance of units was measured and career rewards were given to managers.

Some companies are now explicitly trying to encourage technology transfer across divisions, large-scale development projects that could not be funded within one plant's budget, or integrated product development. A decentralized computer and control-systems company is working to combine devices manufactured by separate divisions into one large system geared to the needs of particular customers. Liquid Tide was developed by three different R&D units at Procter & Gamble working collaboratively across national borders — in the U.S., Japan, and Belgium.

An important goal, then, is increasing the feasibility and legitimacy of such cross-divisional projects.

Conferences, idea exchanges, and "blue sky institutes." Facilitating better information flow across parts of the company and between the company and its suppliers or dealers is one simple way of allowing synergies to be discovered. Rather than one-way information flow characteristic of the command style (a parade of speakers and reports, with highly controlled question and answer sessions) companies are trying to encourage the dialogue and joint problem solving that can generate partnerships through retreats with open-ended agendas.

Overall, the ideal-typical entrepreneurial corporation would be characterized by an integrative culture and structure, one that creates teamwork across any relevant part of the organization, encourages identification with overall company goals rather than "turfiness," and removes barriers to communication or cooperative action. It would minimize hard and fast rules and procedures governed by a rigidly defined command structure and emphasize instead flexibility: broadly skilled sets of employees in flexible units that can be grouped and regrouped as changing circumstances require—or as they spontaneously take initiative to solve problems or create innovations.

In the ideal world, this flexibility and spirit of partnership managed by reciprocity and mutual adjustment would extend to suppliers and dealers as well as to departments considered "inside" the company. Joint undertakings in which both parties work together as a team and exert mutual influence in order to ensure the best joint outcome would be the norm.

A Footnote on "Risk"

Some observers would say that moving to a more entrepreneurial stance requires encouraging more risk taking. But statements like this confuse organizational risk and personal risk, and they emphasize a means or process (risk) rather than an outcome (innovation). American companies do not need more risk. More imagination, more daring, more creativity, more new ideas, yes—but not more "risk." The goal instead is to find ways to get more innovation and entrepreneurship by making it seem less of a personal risk, by reducing the risk to individuals associated with it—and even by reducing the organizational risks by betting less heavily.

In a sense, high innovation companies practice *risk reduction*, not *risk escalation*, with respect to their people's careers. By contrast, perceived risk is naturally high in innovation-averse organizations. When innovation and entrepreneurship are always seen as only a high-stakes game (large bets against large outcomes) there is likely to be less of it. If entrepreneurship means huge investments in very few projects in the hopes of even larger returns, if it means betting one's career on the outcome because "losers" are punished, if it means having to overcome single-handedly years of tradition or layers of bureaucracy or the politics of turf-conscious departments—then innovation and entrepreneurship is indeed very risky. And people reduce their own risks by retreating to conservative solutions.

Under such negative circumstances, I suppose it would seem at first blush like a valid conclusion to desire more risk taking. *But if we instead tackled the root conditions that make innovation risky and in essence reduce the risk, then we are likely to see more potential entrepreneurs opening up new territories and creating new ventures or new systems for their organization.*

What if the "rules for stifling innovation" I proposed earlier were replaced by principles like these?

1. New ideas can come from anywhere. Thus, there is an emphasis on more and better communication, getting lots of information out to everyone and lots of information back.

2. Innovation is legitimate and expected. A portion of every person's responsibility is to look for new and better ways to do things or new and better products to serve their customers (internal and external) and to get rid of the ones that no longer make sense. There is no reason to be afraid to step beyond the job or beyond the department to take responsibility for innovation.

3. People are rewarded for trying to innovate, and celebrated even more for producing a success; but they are not punished for failing.

4. Titles and turf mean less than the ability to contribute, so teams can be put together with any combination of people that makes sense or that entrepreneurs can argue for.

5. There is always something extra available for experimentation, for tinkering, for questioning — uncommitted hours or uncommitted funds or uncommitted equipment, or the flexibility to reallocate them.

6. People at the top are the sponsors of innovation, using the results to help develop the company's over-all business strategy, rather than letting a predetermined course of action dominate everything else.

Conclusion

Analysts of the auto industry agree on one thing: there is no single view of the future because of the complexity of the world industry at a time of restructuring. The problems the U.S. industry faced in recent years are neither transitory nor do they inevitably point to the disappearance of North American manufacturing (Hunker 1983). The future will be determined in large part by managerial strategy.

It is beyond the scope of this paper to suggest specific areas of entrepreneurship for the auto industry; it would be out-of-bounds to even try. Many analysts place a major emphasis on technology and focus on structural realignments in the industy (e.g., internationalization of markets and suppliers, the world car, flexible manufacturing systems, etc.) (see Roos and Altshuler 1984). But this view, while important, is limited. The current strategy of one major manufacturer, General Motors, is highly entrepreneurial: a new venture (Saturn) building a totally new car through new methods and distribution systems with a new organization, and a search for ways to expand its business outside of the industry. And beyond these obvious product and technology domains are additional possibilities for building the business through entrepreneurial spin-offs, small and large, and through innovations in sourcing, servicing, financing, and marketing the core products.

To exploit these opportunities, entrepreneurial management principles will need to spread and take hold. Regardless of the domain in which a business improvement opportunity lies, getting results will be a matter of using a style of management and organization more suited to *innovation and development* than to preservation, more suited to *encouraging change* than to guarding against it. This new mode of management by mutual adjustment *inside* an integrative organization is likely to be matched by a larger number of partnership-type arrangements *among organizations*: suppliers and purchasers, manufacturers and dealers, international joint ventures, joint R&D efforts, and so forth.

Only when participants (employees or whole units) meet as partners, and not as "subjects" in a command structure, is it possible to tap the best of the knowledge of each to make innovations work, and to encourage the maximum cooperation of each to have them established and paying their way quickly.

Earlier in this presentation I offered a minor metaphysical speculation on the question of whether change is possible. I said, in effect, that one never knows until one tries it. But when organization leaders spend much of their time defending against change, finding reasons to avoid it, potential corporate entrepreneurs in those companies have to expend more energy answering the question "Why change?" than moving into action on their projects.

In entrepreneurial settings, in contrast, people do not waste as much time on the analysis and the argument involved in asking "Why bother?". Instead, to paraphrase Robert Kennedy, their byword is "Why not?", and then they prove the opportunities exist by creating them.

REFERENCES

Abernathy, William J., Kim B. Clark, and Alan M. Kantrow. 1983. *Industrial Renaissance.* New York: Basic Books.

Block, Zenas. 1982. Can Corporate Venturing Succeed? *The Journal of Business Strategy* 3 (Fall): 21-33.

_____. 1983. Some Major Issues in Internal Corporate Venturing. In *Frontiers of Entrepreneurship Research,* ed. J. A. Hornaday, J. A. Timmons, and K. H. Vesper. Wellesley, MA: Babson College.

Botkin, James, Dan Dimanesescu, and Ray Stata. 1984. *The Innovators.* New York: Harper & Row.

Darlin, Damon, and Melinda Grenier Guiles. 1984. Some GM People

Feel Auto Firm, Not EDS, Was the One Acquired. *The Wall Street Journal*, 19 December.

Dean, R. C., Jr. 1974. The Temporal Mismatch — Innovation's Pace Versus Management's Time Horizons. *Research Management* (May): 12-15.

Fast, Norman D. 1976. The Future of Industrial New Venture Departments. *Industrial Marketing Management* 8 (November): 264-73.

Hippel, Eric von. 1977. Successful and Failing Internal Corporate Ventures: An Empirical Analysis. *Industrial Marketing Management* 6: 163-74.

Hobson, Edwin L., and Richard M. Morrison. 1983. How do Corporate Start-up Ventures Fare? In *Frontiers of Entrepreneurship Research*, ed. J. A. Hornaday, J. A. Timmons, and K. H. Vesper. Wellesley, MA: Babson College.

Holusha, John. 1985. Toyota Calls Tune in its GM Venture. *The New York Times*, 30 January.

Hunker, Jeffrey Allen. 1983. *Structural Change in the U.S. Automobile Industry*. Lexington, MA: Lexington Books.

Kanter, Rosabeth Moss. 1982. The Middle Manager as Innovator. *Harvard Business Review* 61 (July/August).

_____. 1983. *The Change Masters*. New York: Simon & Schuster.

_____. 1984. Innovation: Our Only Hope for Times Ahead? *Sloan Management Review* 25 (Winter).

Lawrence, Paul R., and Davis Dyer. 1983. *Renewing American Industry*. New York: Free Press.

Macauley, Stewart. 1966. *Law and the Balance of Power: The Automobile Manufacturers and Their Dealers*. New York: Russell Sage Foundation.

Macmillan, Ian C., Zenas Block, and P. N. Subba Narasimha. 1984. Obstacles and Experience in Corporate Ventures. Working Paper, New York University.

Nelson, Richard R., and Sidney G. Winter. 1982. *An Evolutionary Theory of Economic Change*. Cambridge, MA: Harvard University Press.

Quinn, James Brian. 1979. Technological Innovation, Entrepreneurship, and Strategy. *Sloan Management Review* 20 (Spring): 19-30.

Roberts, Edward B. 1980. New Ventures for Corporate Growth. *Harvard Business Review* 59 (July/August): 134-42.

Roos, Daniel, and Alan Altshuler, codirectors. 1984. *The Future of the Automobile*. Cambridge, MA: The MIT Press.

Sakiya, Tetsuo. 1982. *Honda Motor: The Men, The Management, The Machines*. Tokyo: Kodansha.

Schon, Donald. 1967. *Technology and Change*. New York: Delacorte.

Stein, Barry A., and Rosabeth Moss Kanter. 1980. Building the Parallel Organization: Toward Mechanisms for Permanent Quality of Work Life. *Journal of Applied Behavioral Science*.

Stevenson, Howard, and David Gumpert. 1985. The Heart of Entrepreneurship. *Harvard Business Review* 64 (March/April): 85-94.

White, Lawrence J. 1982. The Motor Vehicle Industry. In *Government and Technical Progress: A Cross-industry Analysis*, ed. Richard Nelson, pp. 411-50. New York: Pergamon Press.

Entrepreneurship in a "Mature Industry"

F. James McDonald

I am delighted to have this opportunity to offer some thoughts on one of the most critical questions in management today: How can large, established companies bring into their operations the freedom, enthusiasm, and creativity of the individual entrepreneur?

I framed the question in terms of "how" because I think we all assume that the goal itself is not only worthwhile, but necessary. There is even a new book on the subject, *INTRApreneuring, or Why You Don't Have to Leave the Corporation to Become an Entrepreneur.* The author states:

> The more rapidly American business learns to use the entrepreneurial talent inside large organizations, the better. The alternative in a time of rapid change is stagnation and decline.

It is one thing, however, to set forth abstract principles, and quite another to explain how to use them to create new realities. I will focus this afternoon on implementation, explaining why internal entrepreneuring—or, to use the new term, "intrapreneurship"—has special meaning for us in the car business and what I think that meaning should be. First, we have to confront the question of whether intrapreneurship is possible. There are plenty of nay-sayers and "misfortune tellers," and some executives are skeptical, believing that it can exist only on a token basis. In a recent *Time Magazine* article on this subject, Harold Geneen indicates that it is "the very antithesis of large corporations." He adds that shareholders will never stand for the risks. *Time* goes on to say that the new style "involves a radical departure from corporate policies based on control from the top, layers of reporting and analysis, and an intolerance of failure." And because of that, it will not be easy for executives to "adopt a policy of letting free spirits go off on their own, spending company money with little centralized control."

Furthermore, we have to ask just how far and how literally intrapreneurship can be taken. In the book I mentioned, there was a list of "The Intrapreneur's Ten Commandments." At least two of them—"come to work each day willing to be fired" and "circumvent any orders aimed at stopping your dream"—seem to conflict with the normal needs for personal security and organizational teamwork. As much as we might want to encourage innovation and entrepreneurship, I think we have to admit that not all companies would welcome such attitudes. Also, if we look at the companies where intrapreneurship does work, we find that they already have a tradition of encouraging employees to be independent and innovative by working in small groups.

Another problem for the auto industry is that innovative ideas must be filtered through—and matched against—either specific technical goals or perceived (or probable) customer preferences. Our products are integrated in a way that those of 3M or Procter & Gamble are not. Thus, there is a big difference between gaining corporate acceptance for a new laundry detergent versus, for instance, a new brake system.

The last obstacle is, of course, the one that directly concerns us here. Our industry is "mature" in the classical sense. It has saturated markets and an established technological base. To some, it is mature in another way. I noticed that our pamphlet has quotation marks around the words *mature industry*. Maybe there is something subtle going on there. Could "mature" be a code word for "conservative"? For "rigid," "stodgy," "encrusted with bureaucracy"?

That is, after all, a typical way for large corporations to be known. Decision making by committee, isolation of top management from the real idea generators, reward systems that encourage structured, toe-the-line career paths, a tendency to shy away from new technologies until someone else has taken a chance on them—these are the hallmarks of many so-called "mature" organizations. And that is the way that our business is viewed—all too frequently.

That is, however, not the way we at General Motors view ourselves. Internal entrepreneurship at GM did not start with Saturn. We have been practicing it for some time now, and it is going to be even more of a way of life for us in the years ahead.

To begin with, I think the critics have a point: certain facts of life in older, established companies really do act against the "intrapreneur," especially the more individualistic types—the people that Rosabeth Kanter calls "Lone Rangers." They have, as she puts it, "a strong value orientation" and are "willing to battle the system for what they believe is right, even if they are alone in doing it." Still, we do need people who are willing to take risks, people who are prepared to act on their beliefs, people who know what Thomas Edison meant when he said, "Show me a thoroughly satisfied person, and I will show you a failure." And that is why there is a definite General Motors philosophy of entrepreneurship. Its principles are as follows:

Principle 1: Centralized Policy Making with Decentralized Control

Given the peculiar scope and complexity of our business, top management must encourage innovation without abdicating responsibility. Decentralized control is the answer.

This principle operates in various ways, some obvious to the casual observer, and some not so obvious. Among the obvious examples, of course, is the reorganization of our North American Passenger Car Operations. The goal in this effort is to move products from design to production as quickly as possible. We do that, in part, by moving the decision-making factors as far down as possible and by allowing people more freedom of operation.

In a sense, the reorganization and all that went with it—the new production processes, the decentralized control, the strategic business planning—is entrepreneurship on a large scale. It has big risks, but also big rewards. And it really set the stage for Saturn.

Saturn Corporation will implement a great many innovations. But even now we are getting a lot of cross-fertilization of ideas—which is what we mean when we talk about "Saturnizing" all of General Motors. On the organizational chart, Saturn is a branch of our North American Passenger Car Operations. With that sort of structural alignment, ideas and philosophies can move back and forth very easily while Saturn itself remains a separate, accountable business unit.

Another, less obvious application of Principle 1 is our implementation of Quality of Work Life programs. We have said to our people, "Participative management is vital to the health of our company, but we are not going to tell you how to bring it about." In my opinion, then, the way we go about getting our organization to believe in and carry out QWL is entrepreneurial. You can call it innovative, but it is entrepreneurial as well because we take what we have to work with and come up with new ideas for getting where we want to go.

The same concept applies to the way we are developing product quality: we have set down some quality ethics for all of GM, but each plant, each division, must determine for itself how it will reach the objectives that we've set.

The approaches have also been selected in an entrepreneurial way. Some units have used Juran, some Deming, some Crosby, and this whole process is entrepreneurial on the part of the corporation: we have never used a massive amount of outside consultant work in quality. Yet we are not only keeping the goal in sight but also creating and improvising as we move toward it.

Nor are we just *allowing* and *encouraging* managers to run their own operations. When the business of a division is broken down into small business units and when we insist that managers use business planning, we are actually *forcing* them to be entrepreneurial.

Principle 2: Everyone Is a Potential Innovator

This principle grows out of the QWL concept and the realization that much of the battle for competitive leadership will be won by collecting everyone's ideas and selecting the best of them. The plain fact is that everybody is an expert on how to do his or her job.

Deming notes that "people wish to produce quality; people wish to have pride of workmanship." We take that idea seriously. Our task, then, is to create an environment in which this "quality urge" can express itself in a free flow of ideas, suggestions, and contributions.

Another example of this second principle is simultaneous engineering. Ms. Kanter writes that "the great inhibitor of creativity is . . . the segmented organization, where units work in isolation, mostly indifferent to the efforts and achievements of other units." She is absolutely right. In contrast, simultaneous engineering brings together people from design, engineering, toolmaking, manufacturing, and assembly—as well as suppliers—at the beginning of a project so that everyone can contribute to our achieving the optimum in high quality and low cost and, ultimately, the maximum of customer satisfaction.

Principle 3: Invest, Then Give People the Freedom to Achieve

This principle is most evident in our high-tech ventures – GMF Robotics, Hughes Aircraft, EDS, and the various machine intelligence companies in which we have invested over the last year or two. EDS, of course, already has a highly entrepreneurial culture, and part of the reason we left it a separate entity is that we want to keep that culture intact. On the other hand, machine vision is an emerging industry, and we expect that our investments are going to trigger a major change from development to implementation. But in all of our high-tech ventures, we hope to fan the sparks of entrepreneurialism into a roaring blaze of many new applications.

GM offers proof, then, that a large organization can create a climate in which innovative people and systems can flourish. Admittedly, some ideals are not fully realized. But ideals are like the stars: we never reach them, but like the mariners on the sea, we chart our course by them.

Although intrapreneurship is our focus here, this goal, no matter how brilliant it may be, must not obscure the other, equally critical pieces of a successful competitive strategy:

1. internal reorganization that cuts out bureaucracy and redundancy and makes us ever more responsive to the changing needs of our customers;

2. a global game plan that builds on our own strengths by tapping the resources of others, wherever in the world they may be; and

3. improved labor relations, advances in technology, and people-oriented systems, which, coupled together, give us lower costs and better quality and productivity.

These, along with the fostering of internal entrepreneurship, are our action items for the years to come. We can no more afford to ignore them than the matador can afford to ignore the bull.

Finally, I would add two overriding principles that should guide all of our policies and plans: (1) nothing we can do can undermine the strength of our dealer body; in fact, we should always be working to strengthen it further; (2) nothing we do can interfere with the customer's right to value, quality, and total satisfaction with our products.

As for intrapreneurship, Peter Drucker, who has probably seen every management trend and then some, claims that it is really "just a new name for an old idea." He may be right. The chairman of Samsung Group, in a speech made a couple of years ago, quoted an old Oriental proverb: "If you want 100 years of prosperity, grow men." Today we would say, "Grow *people*," but the thought still stands. And not all wisdom is Oriental. That same speaker said, "American management theories and practices have been a rich source of inspiration. . . . All my success in business owes greatly to them."

I know just what he was talking about, and what I see happening in this country is a rediscovery of the spirit and the drive that gave American business its original and enduring vitality. Meanwhile, inside General Motors, the flourishing of entrepreneurship has created new excitement and confidence, so much so that investments that we are ready to commit for 1987-1989 should not only keep us competitive in the tough worldwide markets that we know and understand, but also, by our forecast, give us the opportunity to serve more people—and serve them better.

Honda's Approach to a Mature Industry

Shoichiro Irimajiri

Among this very distinguished group, I feel like a young man with a very young company. Although I am now approaching middle age, my company, Honda, is still in its youth. As I look down the table at the other members of this panel, I can think respectfully about the long and distinguished history of their organizations. Honda, on the other hand, is *eight* years younger than *I* am.

Yet despite our youth, we have enjoyed some success, in part because of our view that no market is so mature or so difficult that we cannot find a place in it. In 1959 we entered the motorcycle market in the United States. By 1964 we had achieved a leadership position in that market, a position we continue to enjoy both in the United States and worldwide.

We entered the automobile market in the United States in 1970, just a few years after we built our first automobile. Last year we ranked fifth in total sales of automobiles in the United States.

In 1977, long before there was any thought of import restrictions, we committed ourselves to building manufacturing facilities in the United States, and in 1979 we began production of motorcycles in Ohio. We are now first in the manufacture of motorcycles in the United States, both in number of units and in dollar value. We began automobile production at our Ohio plant in November 1982. In 1983 we were the sixth largest manufacturer of automobiles in the U.S., and in 1984, the fifth largest. We are now expanding our automobile facility and expect to be the fourth largest manufacturer of automobiles in the U.S. when it is completed.

In each case, I believe that the market was considered mature before our entry. Or, to say it another way, these markets were considered closed to entry by newcomers.

41

How is it that Honda has enjoyed such success in markets that have been perceived as mature? To understand, you need to understand something about the company. In 1963, when I joined Honda, the company was just fifteen years old. It was not then, and is not today, a typical Japanese company. It has never been a member of a major trading group, and it adopted, early in its existence, a commitment to being an international company. This commitment, for as long as I have known Honda, has been to serve a worldwide market. Although we are first in motorcycle sales in Japan and are constantly strengthening our commitment to automobile sales there, our goal, as often stated to me by Mr. Honda, has been and is to be the best in the world.

Honda is different from other companies in yet another way. We have a complex but well-understood corporate philosophy that is an integral part of our approach to business. Indeed, our approach cannot be separated from our philosophy. Part of that philosophy has always been that our manufacturing facilities should be located in the markets we serve. In the mid-1970s, when we were studying the feasibility of manufacturing operations in the United States, the answer was always the same—it would operate at a loss. Mr. Kawashima, then president of Honda, said, "Go ahead anyway." There is no explanation for that decision other than our commitment to our corporate philosophy, which told us that to serve the American market we must commit our resources to manufacturing in America.

But to understand our commitment to the American market, we must go back even earlier in the history of Honda. In 1959 we established our sales office in this country, known as American Honda. At that time we were basically a manufacturer of motorcycles. We had enjoyed some success in Japan but were already committed to an international sales effort. A key part of the Honda philosophy is that we address our toughest problems *first*. In 1959 no market was tougher for a motorcycle company than the market in the United States. Depending on your point of view, it was either a very limited market or a very mature market, or both.

It would have been far easier for Honda to have gone elsewhere, but Honda's approach was to gain acceptance in the American market first, simply because the American market was our greatest challenge. So we began. In our first year we sold 160 motorcycles in the United States. Four years later American Honda had launched one of the classic campaigns in American advertising history—"You meet the nicest people on a Honda"—and it revolutionized and revitalized the American market. By 1964 nearly one out of every two motorcycles sold in the United States was a Honda, and the once dormant market had been expanded into hundreds of thousands of units a year. Honda had become the leader.

The commitment to U.S. automobile sales and manufacture comes from much the same philosophy. The U.S. automobile market is perceived by many as a mature market with a single dominant company. The conventional wisdom is that you cannot compete with General Motors. We are certainly a tiny little company compared to them, but we believe we can compete by building and selling cars successfully in General Motors's primary market. This, of course, is our toughest challenge to date. Our desire to take on this challenge grows, again, directly from our philosophical belief that we face our toughest challenges first.

Why does Honda believe it can succeed at this challenge? Consider again our basic philosophy: that we must always hold our own torch, that we must develop our own fresh ideas, that we must not copy others, that we must respect the value of research, and that we must proceed always with ambition and youthfulness.

In the early 1970s Honda, then just an infant in the automobile business, was faced with the challenge imposed by the Clean Air Act. In order to meet this challenge, we organized our engineering efforts into teams. I was a member of the eight-man team that came to be known as the "All or Nothing" Team. Our job was to develop an engine that could meet the requirements of the Clean Air Act without the need for a catalytic converter. We had to find a revolutionary approach, and we had to succeed in one year. The result was the compound vortex-controlled combustion (CVCC) engine, the first stratified-charge engine. Our lean-burn engine design was incorporated into a lightweight, economical, sporty subcompact with a unique design, and the CIVIC automobile was born. Had we been satisfied merely to copy others, we might not be in the automobile business today. But, with our new designs, we set the standard for other front-wheel-drive cars, and Honda's automobile business was successfully underway.

The same story of innovation has been repeated many times at Honda. One of the best known examples is our automatic transmission design. Rather than use the patents and technology of others, we chose to develop our own transmission from scratch. As a result, we have a lightweight, fuel-efficient, reliable transmission that is uniquely ours.

Engineering is just one place in which you can see our philosophy in action. Design is another. When the engineers at Honda Research of America identified a gap in the marketplace, they developed a unique concept that became the CIVIC CRX—a lightweight, high gas mileage, sporty, two-passenger automobile. They worked closely with Honda Research in Japan to refine and develop the concept. At its introduction the CIVIC CRX was named the Import Car of the Year by *Motor Trend*. It still has the highest gas mileage rating of any car sold in the United States. Once again, the CIVIC CRX is an example of Honda's belief that we must always find our own way and carry our own torch. That car also stands as an example of how *total involvement* in the marketplace and *teamwork* among all the engineers leads to success. The CIVIC CRX is not a Japanese success or an American success; it is a Honda success, one in which we all take pride.

But what about manufacturing? How does the Honda philosophy work in the factory? After twenty years of experience in research and development and after having become head of motorcycle research and development, I was asked in 1983 to become general manager of the Suzuka Factory, Honda's largest manufacturing facility. At that time, our manufacturing methods were well established, and the managers were very experienced. Was my new job to be merely administrative, without the challenges I had enjoyed for twenty years? It is part of the Honda philosophy to proceed always with ambition and youthfulness, never to accept what is being done simply because it has been done that way in the past, to try always to make improvements. That philosophy applies to manufacturing just as it applies to everything else we do. Every week in Suzuka we made changes, developed new equipment, increased the quality of our product, and improved our working environment. This was not something that was imposed from the top by a group of managers; this was something that grew out of the understanding and application of the Honda approach by our manufacturing associates.

I must admit I wondered what I would find in the United States when, in mid-1984, I was asked to assume the responsibility of President of Honda of America Manufacturing. When I left the Suzuka Factory in June 1984, the average associate had 7.5 years experience in manufacturing automobiles and in applying the Honda way. When I arrived in Ohio, the average U.S. associate had less than a year's experience in manufacturing automobiles. Could they produce automobiles to Honda's standards? Would our approach work in the United States? I think the answer is obvious.

When *Car and Driver* picked its ten best cars of the year in January, it again named the Honda Accord—the one we build in *Ohio*—as one of those ten best cars. *Car and Driver* said simply, "There is nothing wrong with a Honda Accord. Nothing. How many other cars can one say that about?" But why are we succeeding in Ohio? How do we produce quality that impresses even our internal quality auditors when they visit from Japan?

The answer lies in the fact that Honda's approach is to start with respect for the individual associate's intelligence, hard work, and commitment. The signs of our approach are many: we all wear the same white uniform; we all park in the same parking lot without reserved spaces; we all eat in the same cafeterias; we all share the same locker rooms; and my desk, like every desk, is in the same large room with no walls.

But the respect goes far deeper than the tangible signs. First, there is respect between our American and our Japanese associates for what we can achieve together. Our success in Ohio is not a Japanese success or the success of a Japanese company; it is an American success, the success of the American operation of an international company.

Second, our whole approach to quality is based upon our respect for what the individual associate can achieve. We do not mandate quality by having quality inspectors at each step of the manufacturing process. Instead, we teach quality as a satisfying way of life and ask each associate to take responsibility for the quality of our products. If we have a problem, we go out to the floor, look at the actual situation, and ask the associates there for their solutions. There is a saying at Honda that there is more knowledge on the factory floor than in the office, and we have found that the answers to problems and the improvements in our quality and process often do come from the associate who is most directly involved.

In order to make this reliance on our associates succeed, our associates have to understand our commitment to continuous improvement. We have to eliminate the fear of making and reporting mistakes. False pride that seeks to hide problems is one of the greatest barriers to quality. We encourage our associates, therefore, to tell of problems in their areas and then to apply their creativity in solving them.

Third, there is at Honda a certain spirit that is probably best conveyed by the word "togetherness." It is the togetherness we have as members of a team; it is the togetherness we have with our philosophy; it is the togetherness created by shared goals. We believe that if we can create "togetherness" as a basic principle throughout our organization, we will succeed. For almost thirty years that basic principle has been stated as follows: "Maintaining an international viewpoint, we are *dedicated* to supplying products of the highest efficiency at a reasonable price for worldwide customer satisfaction." It is adherence to this principle and to its underlying philosophy that has led us to where we are today. For us, the question is not whether the market is mature or immature. It is not acceptance of conventional approaches and conventional wisdom. For us, it is the knowledge that the future is in our hands. This is our Honda way.

Entrepreneurship in the Supplier Industry

Edmund M. Carpenter

I am pleased to address this forum both as a member of the automotive community and as a representative of ITT. The issue at hand is *Entrepreneurship in a Mature Industry*. I would particularly like to focus on that subject from the viewpoint of an international automotive component supplier.

Let me quickly provide you with some background about ITT and why I have chosen the international dimension. First, ITT is a truly worldwide company, with sales of $14 billion generated in over 200 countries. Corporate business activities comprise such diverse fields as telecommunications, insurance, hotel management, natural resources, and industrial technology. Given this scope, ITT's management team is constantly dealing with research, manufacturing, and marketing issues that cross national boundaries. Perspectives of growth or maturity become frequently evident, demanding unique and longer-term solutions. This implies that we as a team take a positive attitude with regard to changes in any given business environment.

Second, ITT Automotive is an international component supplier serving automakers on both sides of the Atlantic and elsewhere around the globe. Our automotive operations, which are a major part of the $5 billion industrial technology sector, employ some 27,000 people in 70 plants primarily located in North America and Western Europe. The majority of our $1.7 billion automotive component sales is directed to the original equipment sector.

As a worldwide automotive supplier, we, like many of you in this room, have had to wrestle with the fundamental changes in our industry that have completely altered historical manufacturer-supplier relationships. I think it is important to realize that neither

47

peaks nor valleys of future auto industry cycles will essentially change the new direction and demanding business attitudes of our customers. As a result, "survival of the fittest" has become and will remain the name of the game for automotive component suppliers. This is particularly true for the North American environment, where both OEs and suppliers found themselves in the same boat and were forced into quantum leaps for competitiveness against increasing foreign penetration.

It is clear to me that the future viability of parts suppliers hinges on two basic options: to offer a *unique technology*, which is just not available in the same way from anywhere else, or to be *the lowest-cost producer*. A combination of both, of course, is preferable, and a successful supplier will be the one who is ultimately capable of mastering both.

This focus is driven primarily by the need for growth. It implies a clear reading of industry trends and a clear perception of which avenue to pursue, based upon existing and sustainable areas of growth. It also implies a readiness to engage in initiative and innovation — in other words, entrepreneurship.

Last August, I had the opportunity to make a presentation at a management briefing seminar at Traverse City. At that time, I shared my views primarily on cost factors, so let me address the technology issue first. Over the last couple of years, for example, U.S. companies have increased their industrial research expenditures to the point where the industry now spends more money than the government. Spending rates have outpaced inflation rates in an attempt to beat back foreign competition. Contrary to public belief, spending did not slow down during the 1981-1982 recession. A 1984 survey of 800 companies conducted by *Business Week* indicated that 1983 R&D spending levels amounted to $39 billion, up 10 percent from 1982. 1984 expenditures were expected to grow even faster.

These spending trends are indicative of the fact that automotive component suppliers, pursuing high-tech avenues, have to invest in both the engineering capacity and manpower to sustain substantial R&D commitments. Often, commitments are made long before a supplier knows whether he has won or lost a contract. This implies a great deal of risk and demands strong cash resources. It also implies a long-term rather than a short-term return orientation and the existence of what Professor Kanter calls patient funds. Companies that are embedded in multibusiness or multinational organizations enjoy a distinct advantage in this context since they can draw upon the resources of the total corporate R&D activity. This is particularly beneficial in a climate of rapid technological change where product and process innovations increasingly cross traditional national or industrial boundaries. The increased use of nonautomotive technology in automotive applications is but one example (for instance, electronics used in safety or comfort components).

A recent *Industry Week* article predicted that by 1986 a typical car will contain six to eight microprocessors, compared to one or two in 1984. GM forecasts predict up to twenty processor units per car by the end of this decade.

We at ITT Automotive have access to the fruits of a $1 billion annual budget for total corporate research and development, and I would report that the frequent use of nonautomotive technology is not just theory.

A very good example of pooling engineering resources and teaming is the development of ITT Hancock's seat-memory system. Five sister companies in such diverse fields as aerospace, electronics, and defense communications have contributed to the creation of this product. Flexibility and technology transfer have provided us with the opportunity to manufacture and supply the product from several of our companies, according to need and where the application makes the most sense.

Another good example is the ITT Teves electronic brake-control system, one of our new flagship products that was developed by a dedicated team of physicists and electronic and brake-design engineers in Germany. Production start-up was completed in 1984, and initial deliveries to the U.S. began in the second half of last year. When we began this project, we had no commitments from any of the OEs; we began the development with the commitment to increased traffic safety and consumer affordability.

Worldwide demand for this highly engineered system is expected to reach one million units at the end of this decade. By then, certain of the antilock systems will be manufactured by Teves plants in Europe and North America; others will be made under joint-venture agreements with OEs. In some cases, they may be produced under license agreements, one of which was signed with a Japanese company late last year.

We feel that business flexibility will make this product successful in the international marketplace. We will need the volume generated by joint ventures and licensees because of our high R&D

investment. And, while the "antilock" project is being turned over to the application and manufacturing engineers, the Teves development team has begun to embark upon a new major brake development.

I think that automotive OEs value the innovation capabilities provided by their supplier base, and they have begun to secure that very talent. Automakers are increasingly asking for more supplier involvement in the design and development of products, and at very early stages. A good example here is GM's announcement of plans to select suppliers for one of their 1988 car programs, which is approximately two years earlier than usual.

An early selection expresses the need for fast access to technology developments available on an international basis. This is likely to provide suppliers with a reduction of risk, more stability, and sufficient volume once the production award is made. The mutual benefits for both partners are obvious: an early definition of real needs resulting in reduced development time and costs.

One final comment on the technology issue: we should not limit our thinking to the creation of innovative products alone; we must also focus on the process aspects of technology. For example, there is no doubt that a quality- and productivity-driven industry such as ours increasingly depends on new and innovative approaches to the control of manufacturing processes. This is essential and has become an art of survival. Our customers, as well as we suppliers, have learned to demand products that reflect quality without compromise. I predict that any one of us who is not up to speed in statistical methods on the shop floor will not be around much longer.

Recognizing the value of "SPC" implies that we focus on upgrading our systems since they are powerful tools for improvement and elimination of waste. The real strength of statistical methods lies in the motivational power of people; it puts the operator back in the picture and improves accountability. At ITT automotive, for example, we are strongly promoting "SPC" as a basic management tool, not because the OEs demand it, but because we have learned to appreciate its contributions to our bottom line. The same applies to other parts of our corporation.

We have also gone a step further by introducing various methods of statistical experimentation, which are proving to be even more powerful tools in achieving dramatic improvement in cost, productivity, and product quality. After a test phase in 1984 in several of our automotive and nonautomotive plants, we have formally pulled together a dedicated team whose sole mission is to introduce and broaden the use of these advanced methods throughout the ITT system. The team is organized outside of what I would call the ITT corporate bureaucracy: the members are shielded from budget and monthly variance analysis, report writing, and so forth.

We were amazed by the team's findings during the test phase. For example, they established that a large number of the process factors were improperly set by our using traditional engineering methods. In other words, we have not known what made our processes tick. Possibly more important was the fact that substantial improvements in quality, cost, and productivity were achieved with little or no investment. Quite often we learned how to set up our existing equipment to achieve, on average, 30 percent or better improvements in productivity, 10 percent or more reduction in materials, and essentially defect-free quality. One test case in our wire assembly plant yielded the elimination of $1 million worth of planned capital investment and gave the customer a savings of $1 million through the elimination of tests.

This is quite indicative of the benefits new and innovative methods can yield. These tools, promoted through a properly driven program, offer significant opportunity for progress in a very competitive environment. Internally, they have created a spirit of entrepreneurship that is growing not only in ITT Automotive but also in other parts of our corporation.

In summary, I see technology, however defined, as the driving force behind growth in our industry. Component suppliers that focus on the development of unique technologies — and this continent has enormous resources — can develop strong positions on a worldwide basis. Where they eventually end up making or sourcing their products is another question.

Second, I will address the low-cost producer issue that I highlighted as the other major option for automotive component suppliers.

What we see is that the OEs are increasingly leaning toward larger production of fewer model families. This is driven by the need for cost reduction in order to achieve competitive pricing. GM, for example, now produces over 1.5 million "A" and "J" cars per year under various labels. The benefits of manufacturing rationalization, increased component commonality, and a wider dispersal of investments and R&D expenditures are obvious.

The need for cost reduction in turn leads to international procurement of components. As OEs strive to be competitive, they show little reluctance to cross national boundaries once the economics prove to be favorable. Nationality-blind sourcing, which has existed much longer in Europe due to the elimination of customs barriers since the inception of the common market, has gained momentum in North America. Ford Motor Company, for example, is conducting extensive reviews to determine the lowest-cost areas of the world that should be quoted in addition to the home market. This is evidently done to support the development of a strategy for future worldwide purchasing. Interestingly, however, Ford's "low cost" studies seem to indicate a greater correlation between competitiveness and specific suppliers than between various countries.

Another aspect of larger production series is the tendency towards sole sourcing. The OEs have learned that dealing with a smaller group of suppliers results in better and more consistent levels of quality, better purchase prices, and more timely delivery. The suppliers benefit from higher and more cost-effective volume.

We also observe a greater readiness by the automakers to entertain shared investments. This process began in the early 1970s and has accelerated rapidly since. Such moves focus on capital or equity investments and development costs either for car models or joint components. GM's Toyota or Daewoo ventures are examples. Others include Ford's agreement with U.S. Steel to build and operate a $130 million galvanizing plant, and BMW and General Electric have entered into a joint venture to finance BMW's U.S. dealerships as well as to provide loans for dealers' customers.

This trend of OE-OE, OE-supplier, and supplier-supplier relationships is growing. At ITT Automotive, we have several venture proposals under consideration, particularly in the area of advanced brake-system technology.

The objective of these strategies is clear — each partner could not operate as effectively on a stand-alone basis. Partnerships have provided new momentum, and world production of parts and materials has become a reality. In fact, this may have more up-side potential for component suppliers since the same part can go into several high-volume models. The U.S. Department of Commerce, for example, predicts that the OE parts market will grow faster than motor vehicle sales during the next decade.

What do these trends mean for component suppliers? Obviously, larger production runs of same or very similar model families will result in fewer, but very large, contracts of a longer duration. This benefits the OEs because it eliminates multiple sourcing and high procurement expenses. Suppliers benefit from a longer and steadier relationship, cost reduction potential, and longer-term planning accuracy—in other words, a more stable environment. In the case of GM's announced plan to select suppliers now for one of their 1988 car models, it is reasonable to expect that suppliers involved in the prototype design will receive long-term production contracts.

This situation is great for the winners. The losers, however, will be saddled with excess capacity that may necessitate either temporary or permanent shutdown. Suppliers with an international base will find this difficult, expensive, and impossible in some countries.

As a result, competitive pressures will increase, and supplier management will have to demonstrate exceptional navigational and quoting skills. Investment and payback analysis will also be one of the arts of survival. These pressures are supposed to narrow the gap between U.S. and foreign automakers, particularly the Japanese, and they will amplify the industry shake out.

A recent MIT publication indicated that the Europeans may not have as far to go since their cost gap with Japan is narrower. This suggests that the European industry may have a brighter future than the American. However, when looking at both industries today, America seems to be in better shape. Record profits generated by the OEs here have not occurred in Europe, and the cost cutting at both the North American OE and supplier level, which has taken place over the last couple of years, suggests that we may be able to go through the next recession without big losses.

I would now like to focus on some specific cost issues in the context of the international supplier marketplace, starting with some data we had originally collected for that presentation in Traverse City.

The data covers comparative costs of several auto components in the U.S. and potential low-cost sources—not on the much heralded $1,500 to $2,000 per car but on more tangible criteria. The intention here is not to focus on any specific low-cost source or parts category. The point is not in the detail of parts or countries but in the finding that the general U.S competitive position on component pricing is off.

1. Simple aluminum circles are quoted from Japan at 93 percent of the U.S. price.

2. Metal stampings from Spain are 83 percent of the U.S. price; sintered pistons, also from Spain, are 76 percent.

3. Japanese rods are quoted at 74 percent of comparative U.S. price levels, and bearings from the same location at only 66 percent of the U.S. level.

4. Ignition coils from Singapore are offered at 57 percent of the U.S. price.

5. Oil pans from Taiwan are offered at less than half (the exact figure is 47 percent) of U.S. competitive bids, and radiator tanks from Thailand at a mere 40 percent of the U.S. price level.

I have not mentioned Mexico since most of you are very familiar with cost structures there. Nor have I mentioned the People's Republic of China, which may eventually make Taiwan look like a high-cost source.

What causes these apparently wide cost gaps? Differences in manufacturing costs are a function of labor costs. Outsourcing is therefore attractive when labor content accounts for a large proportion of added value. Savings generated must also be measured against the costs associated with moving the part from its point of manufacture to the final assembly process. Certain component categories, however, lean more toward outsourcing than others. In addition, currency fluctuations and exchange rates tend to amplify labor-cost differentials, and the continued high value of the dollar in relation to other currencies is a major obstacle to U.S. competitiveness.

Data pulled together by Labor Department officials, which was published last April by the *Wall Street Journal*, indicates a persistent and widening pay gap between U.S. and foreign wages. Germany, for example, is at 84 percent of the U.S. wage rate; France and the U.K. are at 62 and 53 percent, respectively. Japan stands at 51 percent, and Taiwan, Mexico, and South Korea are around 10 percent plus of U.S. pay levels.

A more specific look at pay rates for motor vehicle workers shows an even wider gap, and this despite major give backs and pay cuts since the last recession. Germany is at 70 percent of pay rates, France at 45 percent, and Japan at 42 percent. South Korea stands at 9 percent.

Although data for 1984 is not yet available, I don't expect to see a narrowing of these gaps given the continued strength of the dollar and the fact that limited wage-increase and concessionary pacts have been reached in a number of foreign industries. Frankly, without the pay cuts agreed to by our labor force, we would be in an even less competitive position.

To avoid the impression of beating on labor, another area of compensation evaluation, supervision costs, also contributes to the U.S. problems. With the U.S. again indexed at 100, Germany is at 80, and Taiwan and Mexico are at the lower end of the scale. A University of Michigan study found that in the U.S. auto industry, for example, the top American executive receives at least 36 times the pay of his top-rated blue-collar worker. In Japan, the ratio is only seven to one. This clearly illustrates that U.S. manufacturers have a problem with the cost of salaried personnel.

Let me now address productivity, the second major cause of differences in worldwide manufacturing costs. Clearly, there are savings to be gained if productivity elsewhere is equal to or higher than that in the U.S. Thus, productivity is a major tool for closing manufacturing cost gaps.

There is a great deal of statistical data available here. Most of it seems to indicate that nothing much has happened to benefit the U.S. In fact, productivity gains in this country have trailed those of other countries.

Data on relative labor costs in the car industries of various select countries published by *The Economist* intelligence unit indicate that when productivity is taken into consideration, West Germany, for example, is at 61 percent of the U.S. level. Japan, at an estimated 40 percent higher productivity rate, is at 33 percent of the U.S. cost level. Mexico is at 20 percent of the U.S. level, and Korea, although only at 90 percent of U.S. productivity, operates at 10 percent of the relative U.S. labor cost.

This leads me to conclude that the current cost gap between the U.S. and low-cost alternative sources is unlikely to be narrowed. Indeed, it may well widen.

This is probably not all bad news for suppliers, particularly those in the U.S., because there are component categories that are sheltered from the low-cost offshore threat. We have already talked about the strength of proprietary technology as a source of protection against foreign competition. Components with minimal labor content due to a high degree of mechanization or expensive material content are also probably sheltered. Finally, transportation is a major factor in the outsourcing equation. Certain parts are just not suitable for long distance shipping due to bulkiness, weight, or other physical limitations.

But what about the component supplier who is directly threatened by low-cost, alternative sources and whose viability and existing investments are in danger. Obviously, that supplier will be faced with a series of strategic options. His decisions must be based on an understanding of where he is in the business and ultimately what he can do best on a sustainable basis.

If, in fact, becoming the lowest-cost producer is the goal, the supplier will have to address outsourcing and/or investing in offshore operations—either alone or jointly—while shrinking expensive capacity at home. This implies a readiness to invest in realignment, that is, locating design, development, customer interface, and manufacturing where it is most effective. This calls for a great deal of flexibility and demands that he toss overboard traditional concerns—"absorption," for example—that have limited entrepreneurial imagination in the past.

There is a caution, however. A bright business idea—a better mousetrap, if you will—does not assure automatic success. A rather compelling statistic bears this out. In 1981, the small business administration underwrote 73,800 loans to embryo entrepreneurs. Only 11 percent of these start-up enterprises exist today.

Perhaps, then, the very word is misleading since the entrepreneurs one hears or reads about are the successful ones. The failed "magnate" or the washed-up "captain of industry" is simply dismissed as one who could not recognize the realities of a marketplace in flux.

The other conclusion is to diversify away from low-cost segments and begin to invest in unique technology. Again, this implies realignment and preparedness to deal with change. Bringing both the cost and technology strands together in our fast-changing international component-supply environment will remain the strategic and tactical challenges of this decade.

Up to this point, I have been speaking to you as a component supplier with a multinational manufacturing base. Let me step out of that role for a moment and speak as a concerned American. As an American I am not concerned about the technology issue because our resources and our ability to excel in that particular area are beyond doubt. What I am concerned about is the future of our manufacturing base in the United States. At hand is the issue of protecting that very base, and a great deal of our entrepreneurial spirit should be directed toward that effort. We must begin to address this topic now—particularly in the good and profitable days—and not when we have our backs against the wall fighting, for example, a 12 percent or greater unemployment rate and social unrest.

We as American managers have a moral responsibility to U.S. society to help guard its wealth and stability. This implies "positive" entrepreneurship with a strong focus on the understanding of the long-term consequences of economic decisions. Positive entrepreneurship, for example, realizes the partnership role of labor and management in problem solving. The past couple of years have shown that both parties are beginning to overcome their traditional adversary position. Entrepreneurship that is short-term oriented and greed driven—as innovative as it may be—is not affordable over the long run.

The Problems of Entrepreneurial Change

Donald Ephlin

Today we are discussing, under the heading of "entrepreneurial change," organizational change in major corporations, principally by bringing entrepreneurship into those corporations. I want to talk briefly about some of the problems that these rapid changes bring to the employees of these corporations and their organization, the union. It is obviously much harder to change very old and successful organizations such as General Motors and the UAW. We keep hearing references to the Hewlett-Packards, Texas Instruments, and companies of that sort, with whom I have a personal relationship while not a professional one. They do not enjoy the benefits of having the UAW in their firms at the moment. They both were described as the best places in America to work and the most successful corporations in America, and then both encountered difficulties shortly thereafter. So, even the small, very innovative, very creative companies in the growth industries run into difficulties adjusting to change. When I consider the change that the auto industry and the auto-workers union have tried to adjust to, then, I think that their task has been much more difficult.

There are barriers to entrepreneurship in our industry. As Rosabeth mentioned, the organization itself is a barrier to change. The union, aside from being a bureaucratic organization like the corporations with whom we deal, is also a political organization — a fact that adds to the difficulty of the situation. Rosabeth mentioned that entrepreneurship means the creation of new combinations; but new combinations to a political group like our international executive board pose a threat. There is resistance. As Rosabeth stated, entrepreneurship requires a system of "management by mutual

59

adjustment, instead of management by command." But, of course, the labor relations system in our country, certainly in our industry, is based on a contractual relationship because of the lack of trust in the early days. When we negotiate once every three years, we try not only to solve the problems we already have but also to write down answers to the problems that might occur two years down the road. Thus, we have become bureaucratic and hidebound at times. Even though in our 1984 negotiations there were more open-ended provisions in our contract because we were trying to build in flexibility and the ability for us to adjust our relationship to deal with the ever-changing situation, such adjustments are obviously difficult to make in our society.

The labor-management relationship between the UAW and General Motors goes back a long time. It started on an individual plant basis; that was the legal requirement in those days. Over the years, then, we have worked together—sometimes it was our idea, sometimes General Motors's—in centralizing many things in order to bring uniformity into the system. As a matter of fact, I made a speech to General Motors executives a couple of years ago concerning the need for uniformity in the application of the labor agreement. But that is now causing us difficulty, because while we have succeeded in bringing everybody together under one contract—something achieved during the boom years of the auto industry—we now have entirely different problems, particularly in the component-manufacturing plants within General Motors.

These problems are due to the higher degree of integration at GM than in other companies. In recent years, we even expanded this centralization. In the past, employees only had plant seniority at General Motors, unless their particular jobs were transferred. Recently, however, hundreds and hundreds of employees have been moved all over the United States to provide them work in new General Motors plants because the changes in our industry have occurred so fast that while one plant was going down, another would be hiring. In fact, our new job security program depends on being able to move people from one plant to another. So, it is not quite as easy in GM as in smaller operations to be entrepreneurial, perhaps. The problems that face us, as an industry and in our mutual relationship, require that we find new approaches to solving some of these problems.

I thought for a moment Mr. Irimajiri was going to steal one of my favorite lines when he said, "We call it togetherness," because our relationship now with General Motors exhibits such a new spirit of cooperation.

Of course—again, quoting Rosabeth Kanter—"there is the need for participants and others to feel that they will benefit if the new unit succeeds." Obviously, this is one of our most difficult problems because people feel challenged and threatened by change, by new approaches—we are, indeed, creatures of habit. We are so large and our relationships have such a troubled history that some of our people are suspicious of the motives of change.

Beyond that, I mention the success of General Motors and the UAW; many people thought we were doing pretty well under the old system and wonder why we are not satisfied to leave things alone. Bear in mind that the union is a reactive organization, and that the union over time will reflect the management with whom it deals. Over the years we have seen changes, and many times management finds it difficult to understand that a political organization like the union takes longer to respond. When it does respond, however, it will respond, when given an opportunity, by making positive contributions.

New approaches require quite a different role for the union and union leaders. Leonard Woodcock hired me to work for the international union many years ago, but not because I was an advocate of quality work life and not because I was in favor of jointness or participatory management—we had not heard of those things. The leadership of the union, coming from the ranks, achieved whatever success they did under the old system. Suddenly, we are saying they have to change to reflect management change. During the recess, one of the people from the media asked me if I thought it was different to work for a GM plant today than it was before. Anybody who has ever been in an automobile plant would have known the answer to that question; the changes we have seen over the years are remarkable.

Within General Motors's section—this applies to Ford, Chrysler, and the other auto companies—we have had tremendous dislocations in our members' employment due to the rapid changes in our product following the energy crisis and the horrible recession. We are faced with foreign competition of a very serious magnitude for the first time in the life of the industry. Right in the midst of this crisis, the entire leadership of the UAW has changed. And then, of course, we have a political climate in the United States that is not very favorable to unions at the moment. Yet when we talk about wage rights and other concerns, it is not because we in the auto industry get too much; it is because others get too little. Real wages in America have actually decreased in the last six years, and that means that the purchasing power of the American people has actually decreased. This is important because we forget that even if we run around the world to the lowest-cost sources for all our products, scoop up all these cheap products and bring them home, no one here will have the money to buy them.

The American labor movement has always been concerned about growth and productivity improvement, but we have also concerned ourselves with sharing in the fruits of that improvement. That has been our creed for many, many years. We have been successful, and we are now working at making the change. But it is not easy to change such a big, cumbersome bureaucracy as the American auto industry or our union. While I was the Ford director, Phil Caldwell one day was very impatient; he didn't think Ford workers understood some economic principle. He was very impatient about it, and I said, "Phil, all you want me to do is teach economics to a hundred thousand people scattered all over the United States, and I can't even get to see them."

The UAW represents 400,000 people scattered in 155 different GM installations all over the United States, and — as in the case of the economics problem — they do not all understand what is happening. One of the reasons they do not understand is because our media does not educate them; it confuses them. Thus, we have the job of trying to get around and explain very complicated facts under difficult circumstances. The task ahead of us is complex, and it requires doing things slowly and gradually.

Again, quoting from our keynote speaker, "entrepreneurship begins by changing in small increments before it effects major changes." We have made strides in changing the way we work together and the way we communicate. One of the requirements for the innovative corporation is to be open, to communicate with people. I have been dealing with General Motors most of my adult life, and the degree of change in some of these areas is such that I am sure people outside the industry could not appreciate it. We have always given advice to the automobile companies, but we used to do it from afar. We would issue a blast from Solidarity House that maybe they heard and maybe they didn't. Now, we do it on a much more constructive basis.

I have on a few occasions in recent years gone to speak with the operating committee — composed of all the operating vice presidents — at General Motors. We did not force them to let me in; it was at the invitation of Jim McDonald. While we don't always agree on everything, we do have the ability now to communicate. At least we are trying to understand each other better and find common ground.

We are also making progress in being entrepreneurs. Magnequench, a new General Motors invention for making magnets, allows GM to make electric motors easier, cheaper, and lighter than before. We are now in the process of working out arrangements to incorporate that job (it will be a relatively small one) into a huge bargaining unit, with some separate applications of the rules so that those motors can be made efficiently in that operation by existing General Motors workers. And the joint venture at Fremont did not just happen; it happened because of an entrepreneurial spirit and hard work. The arrangement that we have worked out there was a great example of the fact that American workers and their American union are not impossible to live with. In fact, I think Toyota management is finding that we are pretty easy to get along with. If we had not worked out the details pertaining to the work force, not only would those Fremont workers not have jobs today, but I do not think that Mazda would be coming to Flat Rock, Michigan, either.

When Rosabeth mentioned that many companies today have set up new venture funds within their organizations for entrepreneurial endeavors, I assumed that few have established them in conjunction with their union. As part of our 1984 agreement with General Motors, however, we have a Growth and Opportunity Committee. Its charge is to look for new jobs that can be created by starting new businesses, new ventures. When this joint committee finds the right kind of new product or new application, money — General Motors has set aside $100 million — can be invested in a new venture that hopefully will provide jobs for other GM workers.

We are doing many things to try to bring about these changes, and the most encouraging part of it to me is not our successes — although I am very proud of what successes we have had — but our attempt to initiate change. Saturn does not represent just some jobs and a plant; it is a statement that we are capable of competing, and that we can be equal to the task of building a popular product competitively in the United States. I have commended Roger Smith and the others at General Motors for the courage to go forward with this project because too much of what we hear today is that we cannot do it. Obviously, I am also proud of the union's involvement, and that Roger Smith went on television before a national audience and, when asked about the union, said, "It would not have been possible to come this far without the UAW and its cooperation. And wherever the plant is located, we will be there together, doing it." That is the kind of spirit we must have.

One of the things that is rather scary in this regard is the fact that when the president of the United States appointed a presidential commission on industrial competitiveness, initially there were no union people on it. Later, he did appoint two of us to serve. But more important than whether or not a union was represented, there was no one appointed from the auto industry. When establishing a committee to discuss industrial competitiveness in the United States, if the auto industry should not have been represented, I do not know who should have been. I joked with Roger Smith: "I not only have to represent half of the labor movement on that commission, I gotta represent the whole auto industry!" However, we did get them to come to Detroit, and we did demonstrate our training programs and made presentations of the Saturn study committee. And none of them had seen any equivalent kind of joint operation. That commission included representatives of Hewlett-Packard, Texas Instruments, and many of the other high-tech companies. They were excited by what they saw happening in the auto industry.

I am very proud of what has happened because over the years the labor relations between the UAW and the auto industry have been among the worst. Today in American society, our relationship is one of the best, and we are working harder to find answers to the problems. We have not solved them all by a long shot. Unfortunately, when we try to work together, we are selling out. But if we don't work together, we are irresponsible. The current situation for labor in America is a lose-lose situation. We're damned if we do and damned if we don't. The criticisms we get when we try to do things that are responsible will not deter us, however. I have to believe that what we are doing in these joint operations is a logical extension of our primary responsibility as labor leaders: to bring about change in the management system, to try to provide job security, and to provide jobs for the people we are privileged to represent. Without those things, all the rest of what we represent would not amount to much.

The high-tech people on the presidential committee, most of whom were from nonunion companies, incidentally, indicated in their report to the president that competitiveness is the degree to which a nation can, under free and fair market conditions, produce goods and services that meet the test of international markets, while simultaneously maintaining or expanding the real incomes of its citizens. Too often in meetings like this one we focus only on why we cannot be competitive, how we all make too much money, and how we can buy it cheaper in Taiwan. We forget that the people we are talking about are also our customers. We are not talking about how many cars can we export to Taiwan, but how many cars they, or the Koreans, or the Japanese, want to bring here. It is our market that everybody is competing for. Unless we can preserve and increase the American standard of living, then we will not have that market, and all our efforts will have been for naught.

The Automobile in the World Economy

Paul W. McCracken

There is really very little reason for those of you who manage companies in the industry to have any remaining uncertainties about the role of automobiles in the world economy. Two major scholarly monographs have appeared on the subject within the last year — one the product of the MIT International Automobile Program, the other the product of the Joint U.S.-Japan Automotive Study under the aegis of the University of Michigan and Technova in Tokyo, and edited by Professors Cole and Yakushiji. Between them, these two volumes represent 543 pages of cogently reasoned prose grappling with the important questions.

In fact, of course, these studies were not even needed. There are numerous matters about which most Americans have quite vague views. Ask a representative sample of the citizenry to give you the names of their representatives in the legislature or the Congress and you will probably get that how-should-I-know look. Ask them about the federal deficit and the response will be more definite. The budget should be balanced, and in ways that involve no increases in taxes or cuts in spending.

Ask an American about cars, however, and that will turn out to be a query in the category of: "Sorry I asked." You will find yourself confronting a person comfortably, even eagerly, wearing the mantle of Ultimate Authority. The fact that no two people will proffer the same advice never disturbs either of them since each knows that he is right. What all of them agree about is that what is so self-evident to them is so obtuse to you in the industry. And as for innovation, "everybody knows" that even Cadillacs and Lincolns could get 50 (or is it 90?) miles per gallon if only you and the oil companies would permit those magic carburetors to be taken out of that secret vault.

Black clouds were hanging low over the world's automotive industry in 1981 when the first of these auto conferences was held. (The weather, however, was remarkably similar.) For one thing, the world economy was itself deteriorating, and at a seemingly relentless pace. This was itself a sharp turnabout from the quarter of a century after World War II when all of the right things seemed to be happening. The O.E.C.D. report of about a decade ago, "Toward Full Employment and Price Stability," pointed out that actual results exceeded even ambitious targets for world economic growth for much of that period. (In Europe and Asia, this document is known as the McCracken Report since I chaired the group of economists; in this country, its existence has been carefully ignored.)

This rapid pace of economic progress was also widely diffused. From 1960 to 1973, for example, output and incomes in real terms were growing at the average rate of 5.6 percent per year even for the low-income countries—a rate that would double total income, in real terms, every thirteen years. This was the figure even for Sub-Saharan Africa (excluding South Africa), where economic vicissitudes have been so severe. Indeed, the so-called developing economies enjoyed a somewhat more rapid rate of economic expansion than the industrial world. The cliche that "the rich are getting richer and the poor are getting poorer" during that period was perhaps good rhetoric for demagoguery, but it was factually incorrect. For all major areas the growth in real output and purchasing power substantially outpaced the rate of population increase, and real incomes were rising persistently.

Table 1
Annual Rates of Growth in Real Gross Domestic Product
(in percent)

Area	1960–73	1982	1983
Developing countries	6.3	1.9	1.0
Low income	5.6	5.2	4.7
Middle income, oil importers	6.3	0.7	0.3
Middle income, oil exporters	6.9	0.9	-1.7
High income, oil exporters	10.7		
Industrial market economies	4.9	-0.5	2.3

Source: The World Bank, "World Development Report," 1984, p. 11.

In addition, the volume of world trade was rising more rapidly than world production. Thus, a growing proportion of output was moving across national boundaries on its way to market. This was also true for the American economy. During the decade of the 1970s the proportion of our production of products (GNP less services and construction) exported doubled, and this was also true for output of manufactured products. This was in important respects evidence of a well-functioning world economy. And it had a beneficial effect on the auto industry. By 1980 roughly 400 million motor vehicles were in use worldwide, about one-third of these in the United States.

Table 2
U.S. Output and Merchandise Exports
(Dollar amounts in billions)

	1970	1980	1984p
Goods GNP	$459.9	$1140.6	$1540.0
Merchandise exports			
Total	42.5	224.3	220.3
Manufactured goods	29.3	143.9	143.1
Mdse. exp. as % of goods GNP			
Total	9.2%	19.7%	14.3%
Manufactured goods	6.4%	12.6%	9.3%

Source: Basic data from the U.S. Department of Commerce.
p = preliminary.

That both the industry and the world economy during the years that followed seemed to take the wrong turn needs no belaboring here. World incomes and output generally, which had been rising steadily at a 4-5 percent per year pace through the first half of the last decade, began to wilt. As we moved into the 1980s, gains in world output sagged further, and in 1982 output in the industrial economies actually declined. Moreover, the volume of world trade declined more than total world output, marking a trend toward international economic disintegration in the literal sense.

This was a period when the Greek playwrights of old would have declared that the Fates had turned against the automobile. In 1979 came the oil crisis, when we made certain by our price controls that most of the world's economic disorder would be concentrated in the United States — another illustration of our considerable ability to shoot ourselves in the foot. And the outlook was as bleak as the contemporary scene. The real price of oil would, we were told, rise indefinitely. This would force a massive shift away from personal transportation, and what cars that would be produced would reflect a severity of design and size that would have brought smiles even to a grim Puritan.

A funny thing then happened to the industry on its way to the industrial graveyard. The road turned in a more positive direction, and prospects are now more encouraging. For one thing, it is clear that no product is in sight that people would prefer over the automobile for their basic transportation. That competition within the industry is intense, and will remain intense, is clear enough. Although it may be cold comfort to a casualty in the market imposed by other producers of cars, there is little evidence of any development in the offing that would make cars themselves obsolete. Those who produce and sell cars do not face the problem of Pickett & Eckel, whose manufacture of high-grade slide rules was doomed not by a better slide rule but by the semiconductor chip and pocket calculators.

There is an important point here. Walter Reuther, in some extemporaneous remarks to the Economic Club of Detroit, put it well when he observed that the automobile represents a fifth freedom. With it people are liberated from the tyranny of bilious conductors and bus drivers, or transit routes not very compatible with where people want to go. Those who are passionately anxious to force our living into a society blueprinted by them, of course, want to containerize us all into buses, street cars, and trains moving along only prescribed corridors. While these people do profess to disdain the automobile, they usually do ride to their protest meetings and cocktail parties in cars — and not stripped-down models at that. More than economics is at work in the fact that most totalitarian societies have a low stock of cars relative to population. Cars give people too much freedom, and that freedom makes totalitarian governments extremely nervous. Czechoslovakia, for example, has less than half as many cars per 1,000 people as Austria. The same comparison holds for East Germany and West Germany.

Predictions that an existing product will not be displaced by something new are dangerous and often turn out to be famous last words. You will recall the manufacturer of steam locomotives who ventured the opinion, as one who had spent his life in the business, that pulling trains with diesel engines would never work. And how could Pickett & Eckel have been expected to perceive, when Bell Laboratories announced the transistor, that this was a death sentence for their slide rules? Yet so fundamentally important to people is personal control of their transportation that the automobile industry's product continues to be secure in the market — at least as long as we avoid political and economic totalitarianism.

A second reason for optimism about the industry's future is that technological advancements are proceeding at a rapid pace. Indeed, the U.S.-Japan Auto Study points out that "innovation is perhaps moving at a faster pace than ever before in the history of the industry."[1] This augurs well for the industry's capability for adaptation to change, at the same time continuing to provide personal transportation. This technological advancement is responsive to market developments, which continue to demand a rich diversity of product offerings. This is an almost inevitable response to rising incomes. The presumption, only a few years ago, that we would all be bumping along in stripped-down little flivvers indistinguishable from each other was clearly off the mark. People differ in their tastes and demands, and this is reflected in the sales and on the highways. Moreover, technological advances in manufacturing enable producers to respond more flexibly to market demands for differentiated products.

Another favorable development, relative to our perspective of only a few years ago, is the discovery that the pricing system works for energy also. At the time of the first of these auto conferences, held against the backdrop of the 1979 oil crisis, "everybody knew" that hanging like the sword of Damocles over the industry would be a chronic shortage of oil and a persistent rise in the real price of gasoline — all exerting a withering effect on the market for cars. That a substantial proportion of the industrial world's oil supplies still comes from the Middle East, where political structures are rickety, is undeniable. If those supplies were shut off because of some political upheaval, the rest of the world would be gasping for more basic reasons than weak sales of new cars. Yet the thread holding that Damoclean sword over us has become at least a cord and perhaps a rope. Market forces do work. Cartels do tend to disintegrate because after members collectively agree to restrict, each then tries to become better off by doing some further business on the side. Higher prices affect the supply side of the market also. If oil was distinctive, it was only that for obvious reasons these market forces took longer to work themselves out and erode the power of the OPEC cartel. (A primary reason was that a major producer, Saudi Arabia, was willing for a time to absorb the cheating of others.) But market forces did work, and we now see the inevitable results of augmented supplies and conservation of demands producing ready availability of products, downward pressures on prices, and a disintegrating cartel.

Perhaps the best news for the industry is that the world economy is once again slowly and fitfully getting back on the path of resumed expansion. Here the American economy led the way. The vigorous expansion in employment, output, and income that got under way at the end of 1982 in the United States clearly pulled the international economic order back from the brink. Whatever problems it has posed for the domestic economy, and they are large, the rapid domestic expansion and the nearly 50 percent increase in U.S. imports during 1983 and 1984 saved the international economic order. It transformed an international debt situation into something merely worrisome instead of something heading us toward a disastrous cataclysm. And it did fuel a quickening of the pace of economic expansion worldwide. While outside the United States 1984 was hardly an ebullient year for the world economy, trends did get started in a better direction. Except for the United Kingdom, major European economies stepped up their rate of economic expansion sharply over that for 1983 and 1982, and real output in the developing countries rose a strong 3.5 percent.

Table 3
Yearly Increase in Real GNP, Selected Areas
(in percent)

Area	1971−80	1981	1982	1983	1984p
United States	3.2	2.5	-2.1	3.7	6.8
Canada	4.2	4.0	-4.2	3.0	4.3
Japan	4.9	4.0	3.2	3.0	5.8
France	3.7	0.3	1.6	0.5	1.8

Federal Republic Germany	2.8	-0.1	-1.0	1.3	2.5
Italy	3.6	0.1	-0.3	-1.5	3.0
United Kingdom	1.8	-1.3	2.3	2.5	2.0
Developing nations*	6.0	2.4	1.5	1.0	3.6

Source: Economic Report of the President, February 1985, p. 356.
*excluding OPEC countries.
p = preliminary.

Furthermore, the present world expansion continues to look solid and sustainable. The debt situation looks less intractable, and price levels are now rising far less rapidly than around the turn of the decade. Consumer prices in the United States, for example, rose 4 percent during 1984, compared with 13 percent during 1979 and an 18 percent annual rate during the early months of 1980. Last year consumer prices in the U.K. rose 4.5 percent, though in 1979 and early 1980 its inflation rate for a time pushed above 20 percent. Industrial economies seem to have learned the fundamental lesson about the importance of maintaining confidence in the future purchasing power of their money.

Here, a critical note about the performance of Japan's economy must be mentioned, and I say that as a long-time admirer and friend of that country. During this critical period, when it has been desperately urgent for imports into the industrial world to expand, Japan has gone full throttle for exports, thereby putting further strain on an already wobbly and disequilibriated international trading order. Japan's trade surplus of $40 billion would be the equivalent of $100 billion for the United States. If the United States embarked on a program that achieved a $100 billion trade surplus, no country would be more outraged than Japan.

If the world economy is slowly and fitfully getting itself established on the path of expansion, and this seems to be the case, the results should augur well for the automobile industry. What influences the demand for cars is a matter that has been studied *ad infinitum* if not *ad nauseam*. Oil shocks, gasoline prices, incomes, credit conditions, employment, prices — these all exert their influence. After reviewing the evidence, however, the MIT study concluded that in "the long run . . . consumers in all developed and newly industrializing countries seem to achieve levels of auto ownership commensurate with their incomes."[2] And based on their assumptions about future rates of expansion for the world economy, the authors project a basic world demand for almost 50 million new cars and 18 million new commercial vehicles per year by the end of the century, relative to 31 million and 11 million, respectively, in 1979—a market growing at roughly 2.5 percent per year. With rates of expansion for the world economy that would be more ambitious, but not out of context with the postwar decades as a whole, this market for motor vehicles could be in the 75-80 million zone by the year 2000.

Table 4
Demand for New Motor Vehicles
(in millions)

Area	1979	2000
New Cars		
Seven auto program nations*	20.50	26.60
Other OECD	4.00	6.50
Centrally planned economies	2.35	4.20
Less developed countries	3.65	11.45
Total	30.50	48.75
Commercial Vehicles		
Seven auto program nations*	5.9	8.7
Other OECD	1.6	2.1
Centrally planned economies	1.6	2.5
Less developed countries	1.7	4.7
Total	10.8	18.0

Source: Daniel Roos and Alan Altshuler, op. cit., p. 115.
*Federal Republic of Germany, France, Italy, Japan, Sweden, United Kingdom, and United States.

Where will these 70-80 million cars, trucks, and vans be made in the year 2000? Here, visibility becomes murky about forces that will shape that pattern. Obviously, economies where cost and quality considerations are unfavorable will lose ground. The tendency in the United States during the 1960s and 1970s for a growing excess of wage rates in the auto industry, over that in manufacturing generally, meant a deteriorating comparative advantage for the American automobile industry. Inevitably, comparative costs have a powerful effect on location decisions. These adverse developments were further compounded by a convulsion of other regulations and laws, often with objectives that seemed to be as much punitive as substantive.

The second set of influences has to do with the nature of the international trading order. Clearly, the liberal, open trading system has been losing ground as a growing proportion of world trade has come to be "managed."[3] The liberal trading order is now on the defensive. Two nations have particularly heavy responsibilities here. While the inordinately high exchange rate of the dollar reflects more than the pressure of large budget deficits on financial markets and interest rates, these deficits are a substantial part of the problem. Correcting that is Washington's problem, and Washington probably has about seven months to fashion a fiscal package.

Japan also must begin to recognize that it has at least as large a relative trade disequilibrium as the United States. The rest of the free world will (and should) take the position that the time has come for Japan to jettison the comfortable illusion that its lopsided external trade is always a combination of virtuous economic policies and performance by Japan and derelictions of economic policies and performance on the part of the West. Japan must start correcting its own huge trade imbalance and realize that direct counteractions by the United States and other nations, such as import surcharges even on a selective basis, must be expected if Japan itself does not take prompt, even draconian action. The distortions that these trade imbalances are imposing on the domestic economy, as reflected here in the loss of agricultural exports and the switch to a huge trade deficit in manufactured goods, will not be tolerated politically, and should not be.

Economic forces are powerful things. Except in totalitarian societies, the demand for personal transportation can be expected to rise as standards of living rise—a trend that itself now seems to be under way once again. The world market will continue to grow.

The fundamental forces of economic progress ought to be moving us toward a growing internationalization of economic life. How that works out for the automobile industry will depend to an uncomfortable extent on whether governments in the industrial world, particularly Washington and Tokyo, can regain a better balance in external trade patterns soon enough to arrest the current trend toward international economic disintegration.

NOTES

[1]Robert E. Cole and Taizo Yakushiji, eds., *The American and Japanese Auto Industries in Transition* (Ann Arbor, MI and Tokyo: Center for Japanese Studies, The University of Michigan, and Technova, Inc., 1984), p. 31.

[2]Daniel Roos and Alan Altshuler, codirectors, *The Future of the Automobile* (Cambridge, MA: The MIT Press, 1984), p. 109.

[3]Cole and Yakushiji, op. cit., pp. 44-45.

Question and Answer Session with Paul McCracken

(Moderated by Robert E. Cole)

Cole: I clearly drew the wrong lesson this afternoon when I indicated that one should never underestimate a wily conservative. I should have noted that it's best to provide Paul with a gracious introduction. He made some stirring remarks. Now, in the time we have left, he will take questions from the audience.

Were the voluntary restrictions on Japanese imports good public policy? What would have happened without them?

McCracken: Economic policy in the domain of government very frequently attempts to find the optimal second-best course of action. I suspect that voluntary export restraints, given the situation at the time, were about as good as what could have been worked out. What would have happened without them? Well, it's easy to conjure up an image of a deluge of cars that would have inundated the American market. On the one hand, I suspect that imports of Japanese cars would have been larger than they were. On the other hand, Japan would have been no more interested than we in creating a tidal wave that would have swamped our market. I suspect that *de facto* there would have been quietly something like the import restrictions anyway. I suppose a variant of that question is: Given what seems to be shaping up, how much will imports increase now? Well, you have all heard estimates of this. My estimate — I might add, an estimate in which I have absolutely no confidence, but I have no confidence in anybody else's estimate either — is something like 300,000 more vehicles.

Cole: You proposed possible surcharges on imports by the U.S. if Japan does not control itself. Is this a change in policy position for you?

McCracken: I did not propose it; I said this is going to be coming down the pike if we do not get this thing straightened out. Nor would I propose it. For one who has had an orientation professionally in the direction of a liberal trading order, it would be very difficult for me to propose something like that. I did, however, want to cite that as something that might be realized if some discrete event of an unfavorable nature created pressure in Congress. Early in 1971, if somebody had said, "I predict that before the year is over we will have an import surcharge levied," I think all of us would have said, "That's ridiculous." But in mid-August 1971 we got one. A concatenation of circumstances developed that caused drastic action to be taken. A chain of unfavorable events today could also produce drastic action.

Cole: Can you illuminate this audience with a final conclusion on the subject of whether or not the Japanese government is manipulating the value of the yen?

McCracken: This issue has been looked at very carefully, and there is no evidence that Japan is manipulating the value of the yen. Rather, the exchange rate is the end result of a whole concatenation of trade and other policies that have produced a disequilibrium in trade. The Japanese can respond, and very rightly, that to an important extent this problem is an American problem, an America-made problem incident to our fiscal policy, and they would be on strong ground. The basic reason I wanted to speak rather plainly here tonight was that I have been observing these developments over a long period of years, and the problem always seems to be something that the United States is doing. I sense, however, that the tolerance for this kind of one-sided diagnosis is wearing a little thin. My advice to my friends in Japan is that we are much closer to some kind of action that will accelerate the tendency toward more severe "management" of international trade than we have yet seen. Certainly, that is the sentiment in many countries in Europe, and it's the ruling sentiment here. The proportion of world trade being managed has been rising persistently, which is an ominous sign, and one of the economies that would be most severely affected would be Japan's.

Cole: What specific economic and trade policy changes should Japan initiate in order to reduce her disequilibrium?

McCracken: Here, I have a very easy answer. Fundamentally, there needs to be a program that aims at redressing this imbalance and, at the same time, providing the foundation for turning the international trading order around and having it start to move once again in the direction of a growing internationalization. How that is to be worked out is, to a substantial extent, for Japan to decide. From the standpoint of the rest of the world, what will be watched are the results.

Cole: Do you not think that the value of the dollar and the interest rates are being kept artificially high in order to fund the budget deficit via the use of foreign capital?

McCracken: Well, in a way, the answer to that question is yes. But as I have often said, you do not survive in academe with short answers. I would not say that interest rates are being kept high in order to finance our requirements. Rather, I would say that the pressures of demand against supplies in the credit markets tend to force interest rates to a level where this country becomes an attraction for foreign savings. Bear this in mind, that the foreign saver has all of the risks that the domestic saver has, plus one more — a foreign exchange risk. There is a risk to the Japanese saver; if he puts $1,000 at work in the American capital market now, it will cost him roughly ¥260,000. Now, however, he has to reckon with the risks that the dollar might weaken. After all, the yen in the last ten years has been as strong as ¥180 per dollar. So a real risk exists even if he hedges his own position. It is not so surprising, then, given this pattern of treasury and private demand pressing against a supply of domestic savings, that we have pretty high interest rates.

Cole: Maybe this is a good question to close our forum: You made a good case, an elegant case, for the survival of the car as a personal mode of transportation and for the economic recovery, but you seemed to finesse the issue of how much of that production will be located in the United States. Could you be more specific?

McCracken: Gee, I feel flattered that I finessed that. Well, I did, of course, cite some figures about the size of the market as we looked down the way. I suspect that the percentage of the world automobile industry located here — by located "here," we mean produced here — will continue to edge downward. But that is not decreed by the gods, and how it all works out depends on what we do.

Cole: I hope it was a productive day for all of you; thank you for joining us at the University of Michigan.

PART II: ISSUES FOR DEBATE

Policy, Corporate Ideology, and the Auto Industry[1]

Taizo Yakushiji

Introduction

Beginning four years ago I participated with other Japanese and American scholars in the Joint U.S.-Japan Automotive Industry Study, whose report was published in 1984.[2] Throughout the study and in the report itself there were two important assumptions. The first was the recognition that the automotive industry has not yet arrived at a mature stage. It is still possible to fill new market niches by introducing new technology-led products. That is, the success of the automotive industry hinges on its ability to introduce a technologically improved or innovative car that will suit the taste and aspirations of consumers.

The second assumption was that in discussing the problems of the automotive industry, two types of problems must be clearly differentiated. The first type might be called macro-political, including, for example, the level of economic prosperity, unemployment, energy crises, and exchange rates. The others are industry-intrinsic issues, such as productivity, quality control, and the reduction of manufacturing costs. The question with which I begin this essay is: Do these two assumptions still hold today?

The importance of this question is emphasized by several recent developments. These include:

1. On 19 February 1985 the U.S. Government's Cabinet Council for Commerce and Trade decided not to ask the Japanese government to extend the Voluntary Restraint Agreement (VRA) for a fifth year, starting in April 1985.

2. The General Motors Corporation announced its Saturn Project and attracted considerable enthusiasm by arousing almost nationalistic sentiments among American consumers. It also announced the purchase of two high-tech companies, Electronic Data Systems and, more recently, Hughes Aircraft. Other competitors are rumored to follow this move by GM.

3. Korean automotive manufacturers, particularly Hyundai, are now scheduled to enter the U.S. market with the 1986 model year. This is a deliberate next step following their successful entry into the Canadian market.

4. The U.S. ran an unprecedented trade deficit of $123 billion in 1984, of which nearly one-fourth is due to the deficit with Japan. Prospects for 1985 look even bleaker.

5. MITI's Minister Murata announced at a press conference on 28 March that Japan would continue the current export quotas, but with an increase of 450,000, to amount to total annual exports of 2.3 million units. Later, on 11 April, Prime Minister Nakasone said in the Diet that most of these increases would be allocated to captive imports for GM (Isuzu and Suzuki cars) and Chrysler (Mitsubishi cars). Nakasone also regretted the bad timing of Japan's announcement on quotas and said that the lateness of the decision triggered additional conflict in U.S.-Japan trade negotiations. It is quite rare in the environment of the Japanese government for a prime minister to condemn an agency's actions. This indicates the existence of interministerial conflicts within the Japanese government over trade matters.

In the light of these developments, it is important to focus on the following three issues: first, the logical dilemma faced by the Japanese government as it attempted to deal with the American termination of the VRA; second, the homogenization of corporate strategy, an *effect* of the VRA; and third, the question of "competitive edge," particularly for the American automotive industry. No final answers are possible, but some speculations about each of these issues can be made.

Protectionist Backlash and Boomerang Logic

Japanese observers of the automotive industry still remember an article by a high-ranking MITI official about four years ago.[3] In a newspaper op-ed piece, he tried to explain MITI's position with regard to its newly instituted restrictions on Japanese automotive exports. At the time, the Japanese public was sympathetic with the position of the Japanese automotive companies, who claimed that the increase of Japanese auto exports to the U.S. was not the result of irresponsible export thrusts but the fault of American manufacturers who could not meet the new demands of American consumers caused by the two energy crises. He called this mood of the Japanese public "soap nationalism"[4] and said that it must be overcome. Export controls would be required to counteract American nationalism, a nationalism that goes back as far as the Boston Tea Party in 1773. Continued high export levels would lead to a protectionist backlash on the part of the United States. If the Japanese automotive industry and the public would understand this higher national priority, the relationship with the U.S. would be harmonized, and Japan's national interest served.

It is a striking fact that MITI was once again worried about a protectionist backlash from the United States with the termination of the VRA. The rationalization employed by the Japanese government for the 1981 VRA was to avoid protectionist backlash, but the same logic was applied when the VRA was being terminated this year. Does this mean that MITI's logic was flawed back in 1981? Did the concessions made by the Japanese auto industry appease American nationalism, or instead did it exacerbate the situation?

There is at least one clear difference between the two situations, however. In 1985 the American target was not really Japanese exports, but imports. What the Americans really wanted—and still want—was open access to Japanese markets for four commodities: telecommunication equipment, electronics, lumber products, and pharmaceuticals and medical equipment. That the Americans did not ask for an extension of the auto export quotas was a clever tactic, a trade-off to pressure Japan to open its markets. Considering the automotive profits of $9.8 billion in 1984 and the unpopularity of the VRA among American consumers, this tactic was quite opportunistic and may be quite effective.

In fact, the Japanese government seemed to fall into a dilemma. The risk of exciting a protectionist backlash among Americans was actually much higher earlier this year than in 1981. Therefore, the government recognized that something should be done to restrain exports, particularly automobiles. However, this time it could not use the "backlash" logic to justify its actions to the Japanese public and the industry. If it used the backlash argument, there would have been two sets of undesirable consequences. One set would have been at the practical level. Many would have said that Japan instead should have opened up its market because this would have been the best response to American protectionism. Moreover, holding down auto exports today would have upset American consumers, who have already been complaining about the price increases in automobiles that were caused by the VRA. Finally, there would have been the danger of a possible antitrust suit by American import dealers if MITI had tried to restrain exports through covert administrative guidance, or if Japanese auto companies had reached a "spontaneous" cartellike agreement to control exports on their own. The other set of consequences had to do with MITI's position in Japan. If MITI officials repeatedly had used the same logic for a policy measure even when the basic situations were different, the public would have had the impression that Japanese trade policy was inconsistent, and would have thought that it was in deep trouble. That would only have made the formulation and implementation of policy responses more difficult in the future.

The result was that MITI could not take any drastic actions, but simply keep the same VAR, plus a political flavor of allowing more captive imports for the American manufacturers. This was in opposition to Reagan's earlier decision and equally disappointing to American consumers. In this regard, Nakasone's regrets, mentioned above, reflected the dilemma of the Japanese government and of MITI in particular.

This analysis suggests that justifying export restraints by pointing to nationalism in the importing country may be very persuasive and effective, but it is also very risky. The logic can boomerang, giving the importing country the chance to take over the same logic to try to impede exports of *other* commodities, and even to strike back and gain market access in the exporting country. In this sense, it threatens not only the competence of the policymakers but of the domestic industry itself.

In a deeper sense the applicability of this "backlash logic" may depend on the degree of maturity of the industry in question. If it had been true that in 1981 the American auto industry was mature, the "backlash logic" might have been justified since Japanese automotive exports clearly would have threatened the takeover of a key industry, one on which the lives of Americans depended. In this sense, MITI's reasoning in 1981 implied that Japan was viewing the American auto industry as already mature. However, the unprecedented profit levels in the American auto industry in 1984 clearly indicated that the industry was not mature. Thus, the only rationale for the VRA was competitive trade policy. It was a limited program to assist the American industry to regain its competitive edge, and it rested on the assumption, mentioned above, that the industry's inherent problems must be separated from the macro political and economic issues at the national level.

If this premise had been stated clearly at the outset, when the VRA was instituted in 1981, Japan might be in a better position to avoid "boomerang" counterattacks from the United States. This observation points up the dangers of the "umbrella" concept, which is a typical negotiation tactic to deal with all possible issues at once. The problem with that concept is that it is difficult to draw a line between what are negotiable exports and what are not when an economy is evolving dynamically.

Corporate Strategies

In the late 1940s and early 1950s there was a confrontation among prominent economists and industrialists in Japan regarding the development of the Japanese auto industry. The debate centered on economic versus technological issues. Economists argued that since Japan had already fallen far behind the rest of the world in manufacturing automobiles, it would be foolish to build up the auto industry again. Substantial amounts of the industrial materials that were needed to reconstruct the war-devastated economy would have to be used. Theoretically this argument made good sense, so many economists and economic planners supported it. On the other hand, a minority argued that an automobile uses more than 30,000 parts. Therefore, rebuilding Japan's auto industry was not simply a matter of building one industry but of enhancing the technical capabilities of other peripheral industries. The minority argument finally prevailed, and the result has been that Japan now has nine competing auto companies that are renowned around the world for their superb manufacturing technology and their effective penetration of overseas markets. This was the victory of a technological logic based on the dynamics of change over an economic logic based on simply an evaluation of economic efficiency at a given point in time.

The implications of this history are important today. Imposition of the VRA led to the homogenization of corporate strategies among both American and Japanese auto firms, and it facilitated the entry of heterogenous companies from the NICs, especially Korea. The explanation for this effect is straightforward. The VRA increased the average price of imported cars from Japan. Because the ceiling was on the number of units rather than the dollar value of sales, Japanese manufacturers upgraded the automobiles they exported so as to maximize their profits. Average prices therefore increased. This effect can be observed particularly for those companies that had relatively small shares of the export quota. Naturally, a market vacuum was created that opened an opportunity for the Koreans, other NICs, or perhaps Japanese secondary manufacturers to export through American auto firms.

Again, the creation of this vacuum is due to the fact that American and Japanese auto firms have increasingly come to share similar corporate strategies that emphasize cutting waste or organizational slack.[5] Both American and Japanese manufacturers lean more and more toward economic rationality.

It is important to remember that the real reason for instituting the VRA was to give American manufacturers breathing space so they could regain manufacturing productivity and their technological edge. The logic was technological rationality, not economic rationality. Nonetheless, the result was economic. The many reports that one reads today about the impact of the VRA corroborate this point. These are devoted almost exclusively to economic issues and neglect the impact on the technological side. Therefore, people are misled about what the results of the VRA were supposed to be, and everyone focuses completely on economic cost/benefit arguments.

Looking more closely at the Japanese case, we observe that in 1984 Japanese domestic auto sales dropped by 9.8 percent. However, total sales including exports went up, thanks to the successful campaign to sell small trucks in the U.S. The implication here is that the U.S. market progressively is becoming more vital to Japanese producers. Today, Japan's auto firms face the two agonizing facts of stagnation in their domestic market and an increasing dependence on the American market. This situation is similar to that faced by Japanese color television producers in the late 1960s. The response of Japanese automakers to this situation is in fact quite similar: to develop their own overseas production facilities, whether or not the VRA remains in place. Honda's increased production at its Ohio plant, the new Fremont operation undertaken by General Motors and Toyota, Mazda's decision to build a new plant at Flat Rock in Michigan, and Nissan's initiation of passenger-car production in Tennessee are all important signposts of this new direction.

However, not all of the nine Japanese auto companies are able to produce cars abroad. Some of them will have to pursue their own international strategies under the oligopolistic structure of the automotive industry. I am referring here to the secondary and tertiary companies that receive a relatively small share of the export quota. What will they do? First, the stagnation of the domestic market has produced equal hardship among all manufacturers, wherever they stand in the oligopolistic hierarchy. Second, the primary group of companies, those with the larger shares, could ameliorate their situation by making higher profits in overseas sales, thanks to the VRA. Third, the smaller companies therefore had to develop their own unique strategy to survive, one that distinguishes them from the giants they compete with. The only strategy available was to introduce a competitive car through technological innovation.

In other words, the VRA has intensified the cleavage between the economic-minded larger corporations and the technology-minded smaller automakers. Of course, the differences are not so clearcut: both types of companies can rightly claim that they follow both strategies. Moreover, Schumpeterian economists might argue that the profits gained through the VRA-controlled export sales would provide larger firms with more opportunities for technological development since they can invest more money in research and development. GM's recent purchase of EDS and Hughes might be seen as corroborating this argument. However, as has been indicated by the recent controversy over the high bonuses paid to American auto executives, in reality, in a more comfortable economic situation, companies are not likely to try as hard.

Competitive Edge

At the fifth U.S.-Japan Automotive Industry Conference at the University of Michigan, Donald Ephlin of the United Auto

Workers made an interesting comment.[6] He wondered why executives from the automotive industry were not represented on the Presidential Commission on Industrial Competitiveness, which was chaired by John Young[7] of Hewlett-Packard. Mr. Ephlin joked that his membership made him feel that he had to represent the entire auto industry.

Membership of this commission is comprised of individuals mainly from the so-called "high-tech" industries. It also includes labor union leaders, university professors, bankers, and lawyers. This commission is the same sort of phenomenon as the Department of Energy, created by President Carter in response to the energy crisis. That is, it is an attempt to respond to the American high-tech crisis through institutional measures. The commission's report therefore proposes many institutional ideas ranging from creating a Department of Science and Technology or a Department of Trade, to modifying the Anti-Trust Law, the federal loan program, or tax laws, strengthening export controls, and implementing various educational reforms, and so forth.

An obvious question is, Where does the American automotive industry fit in? Is it a leftover, separate from the next generation of high-tech industries that are the real stakes in today's trade battles.[8]

If the American auto industry had not recovered so spectacularly during 1983 and 1984, it is very likely that its executives would have been included in the commission's membership. That is to say, the inclination of the American government is to use "surgical" measures, policies aimed only at troubled industries, rather than "preventive medicine" treatments for sustaining key industries. American industrial health is to be regained by implanting an artificial organ, like a new government agency, creating a new bypass for the passage of financial "blood," or stopping a hemorrhage by sewing on the much stronger tissue of export controls.

This clearly seems to be the basic pattern of American governmental intervention into industry. Attention goes to the "sunset" or troubled industries, those that are malfunctioning and seem likely to die. Perhaps this pattern is from motives of fairness, or because only such interventions can be legitimated in American politics; of course, the impact of declining industries on unemployment accelerates this tendency through generating mass political pressures.

To make an almost tautological statement, however, competitiveness can only be maintained through competition.

Normally one thinks of competition as a sizable number of roughly equal independent players competing among themselves. It might also be argued, however, that some Western countries and Japan have achieved a different form of competitiveness, which might be called "state-driven" competitiveness. The recent report by the National Academy of Science makes this argument.[9]

Yet it is misleading to equate such state-driven competitiveness with the American "surgical" approach to industrial policy mentioned above. As the report of the Joint U.S.-Japan Automotive Study indicated, the Japanese government created institutional arrangements of this sort, but these were generally "preventive-medicine" oriented. They were aimed not at curing a sick industry but at insuring that its weakest organ would be able to function normally. That is, the problem of the postwar Japanese auto industry was to maintain its health during a period of rapid development. What was needed were measures limited in time and focus: namely, strengthing the small- and medium-sized companies in the auto supply industry. When these suppliers were able to function at adequate levels, the treatment was stopped.

In general it is probably true that the "preventive-medicine" sort of industrial policy implies an emphasis on "peripheral" industries, those that support the key industries. Jacques S. Gansler pointed out that the U.S. is facing serious competitive problems even in the defense industry because the government has tended to focus only on the "surface" or "summit" industries and has neglected the peripheral industries.[10] He is not the only observer who has recently called attention to these supporting industries. Others include William Abernathy, who writes of the "productivity dilemma,"[11] Burton Klein, who argues for "dynamic efficiency,"[12] and many more. There are good reasons to emphasize the importance of highly competitive peripheral industries. They are more "dynamically efficient" and less oriented toward "scale-of-economy." They therefore focus on *innovation*, and innovation at the periphery supports the competitive position of the entire industry. If policy is directed only to "surface" industries, the emphasis is likely to be on more productive and profitable operations in the economic sense; that is, organizational slack is often eradicated, which may in fact diminish the rate of innovation. It is sad but true that innovation may often flourish under an uneconomic or inefficient managerial regime.

This entire question actually has an international political dimension. America's "surgical" approach to industrial competitiveness may reflect her long-standing leadership in the free world since the end of World War II. In order to secure the hierarchical order of the free world regime, America has had to maintain political, economic, and technological supremacy over the allied countries. This has required American industry to monopolize quantum leaps of innovation in the frontier fields. Such quantum leaps require a slow-moving technological random walk, a process that is very expensive. The necessary huge investment in these frontier areas can only come by emphasizing high profits — an economic logic — in the other areas. One such area is the American auto industry, which in this sense has played a major role in maintaining the postwar liberal regime.

This perspective on the international political economy is perhaps the ultimate reason for the resource-generating and economizing corporate strategy of American auto manufacturers. The intensive search for offshore sourcing and competitive bidding with economically superior upstream and downstream suppliers are two good examples. On the one hand, these exemplify the American orientation toward economic efficiency; on the other hand, if William Abernathy's thesis of the "productivity dilemma" holds, it is also likely that American technological strength is being transformed from prime contractors to the offshore companies that supply them. When these foreign companies gain technologically, their progress helps American companies to gain still higher economic efficiency, which is exactly the ultimate objective of the hegemonic nation — the U.S.

But is it possible for the American auto industry to rise from its current worker-bee role and appear as one of the nation's frontier industries? This depends on internal efforts by the industry itself, since clearly the American government's orientation will not be helpful. As has already been explained, however, the impact of the VRA was to emphasize economic efficiency. This is fine from the government's point of view because then the American auto industry can continue to serve its resource-generating function for the entire nation. There is therefore considerable inertia in regaining the industry's competitive edge. In my view, the question of whether the industry can successfully combat this inertia is not an empirical issue; it is essentially an ideological one.

Conclusion

I have tried to be provocative in this essay because most discussions of the VRA have focused on economics and have ignored policy. My argument is essentially normative. That is, I have emphasized the importance of both government policies and corporate strategies. The impact of the VRA has been to accelerate the emphasis on economic efficiency rather than technology. This occurred in both the American and the Japanese auto industries—and indeed on the part of both governments—with the possible exception of smaller firms in Japan and Korea.

The points that I think should be more seriously considered are in fact the two assumptions of the Joint U.S.-Japan Automotive Study. First, technologically speaking, the automotive industry is not yet mature. Second, the problems at the macro political and economic levels and at the level of the automotive industry itself are separate. I have not tried to offer a comprehensive analysis, but I believe that these two assertions provide a good starting point for future discussion of the competitiveness of the American automotive industry, and the evolution of the U.S.-Japan economic relationship.

NOTES

[1]The author is grateful to Professor John Campbell for his critical comments on the earlier version of this paper. Opinions expressed herein do not necessarily represent those of research and policy members of the Joint U.S.-Japan Automotive Study. I take responsibility for any errors that may appear here.

[2]Robert E. Cole and Taizo Yakushiji, eds., *The American and Japanese Auto Industries in Transition* (Ann Arbor, MI and Tokyo: Center for Japanese Studies, The University of Michigan, and Technova, Inc., 1984).

[3]N. Amaya, "Jisyukisei ni tsuiteno Tsusansho no Kangae," *Nihon-keizai-shinbun*, 1 June 1981, p. 14.

[4]N. Amaya, "Soap-nationalism o haisu," *Bungei-syun-jyu*, July 1981, pp. 318-38.

[5]This means an increase of Leibenstein's X-efficiency; see Harvey Leibenstein, *General X-Efficiency Theory and Economic Development* (Oxford: Oxford University Press, 1978).

[6]See Donald F. Ephlin, this volume.

[7]*Global Competition: The New Reality*, Report of the President's Commisssion on Industrial Competitiveness, January 1985.

[8]*Business Week*, 11 March 1985, pp. 56-67.

[9]*The Panel on Advanced Technology Competition and the Industrialized Allies* (Washington, DC: National Academy of Science and National Research Council, 1983).

[10]Jacques S. Gansler, *The Defense Industry* (Cambridge, MA: The MIT Press, 1980).

[11]William Abernathy, *The Productivity Dilemma* (Baltimore: Johns Hopkins University Press, 1978).

[12]Burton H. Klein, *Dynamic Economics* (Cambridge, MA: Harvard University Press, 1977).

White Collar Human Resource Management: A Comparison of the U.S. and Japanese Automobile Industries[1]

Vladimir Pucik

This article explores the role of Human Resource Management (HRM) within the Japanese and U.S. auto industries. The white collar labor force characteristics are discussed in the context of specific HRM functions. Implications for future HRM policies are considered.

At present white collar employees comprise nearly one-third of the total labor force in the American and Japanese automobile industries. Their ratio is expected to increase during this decade, stimulated by the shifting structure and content of jobs brought about by technological change. In this environment, an effective management of white collar human resources becomes one of the key conditions for long-term success in the world's auto markets. For example, within the engineering function, which constitutes probably the most critical area of white collar employment in the auto industry, increased technological sophistication and the complexity of both the final product and the manufacturing process will require large numbers of qualified technical employees to maintain and improve the competitive position of each vehicle manufacturer, as well as their suppliers.

Recruiting, developing, and motivating this group of employees is already one of the most critical tasks facing the auto industry today. However, most of the recent discussions concerning the current competitive position of the U.S. and Japanese automotive industries and their prospects for the future focus mainly on issues related to blue collar workers, their productivity, wages, and labor-management relations in general.[2] In contrast, the issues concerning the roles of white collar employees, in particular managers, supervisors, and technical professionals, have been analyzed only sporadically.

In this context, the objective of this article is to present a comparative review of current conditions of white collar employment in the U.S. and Japanese auto industries, with particular emphasis on corporate Human Resource Management (HRM) policies. The article begins with an analysis of white collar labor force composition and demographic profiles. It will then discuss the role of the personnel function and specific HRM functions targeted at white collar employees. It concludes with a summary of current trends and their implications for future HRM policies.

White Collar Labor Force Composition

The proportion of white collar labor force[3] in the total labor force is similar for automotive firms in both countries, ranging from 26 to 33 percent (table 1). Among parts suppliers in both countries the proportion of white collar labor is slightly smaller, 24 to 29 percent depending on size. Some of the differences in these figures can be accounted for by differences in job classifications at the interface between white collar and blue collar jobs. However, especially in the case of the U.S. firms, differences in "lay-off" policies in a retrenchment period may also play a role, as pointed out below.

Table 1
White Collar Labor Force
(percent of total labor force)

	U.S.	Japan
White collar employees (WC)	26-33	29-33
Managers and supervisors	10-11	7-9
Technical staff	6.5	14
Financial staff (% of WC)	8-10	1.5-2.0
Levels of management	12-14	7-9

In the U.S. firms 68 to 72 percent of the white collar labor force are salary-exempt employees. Among these about 32 to 37 percent are placed in supervisory and managerial positions, accounting for approximately 10 percent of the total labor force.

However, only about one-tenth of supervisors and managers are eligible for an incentive bonus, a distinction of considerable importance. In Japan the ratios are again similar, although direct comparisons are difficult not only due to differences in job classification but due to the exclusion of female workers from a number of personnel statistics. In Japanese company Z supervisors and managers (including employees of equal status without managerial responsibilities) account for 8.2 percent of the total labor force. In Japanese company X the number of managers equals just over 3 percent, or 13 percent of white collar employees. About 75 percent of these are ranked as section managers. The remaining 25 percent of managers occupy one of the three higher nonexecutive ranks.

Although the ratio of white collar to blue collar employees is comparable in the auto industries of the two countries, differences appear when the employees' occupational classes (e.g., technical or nontechnical employees) are also considered. In Japan the proportion of engineers and technical support personnel reaches, on the average, nearly 14 percent of total employment (7.6 percent engineers, 6.2 percent technical support). In the U.S. the total engineering share is only 6.5 percent (4.1 percent engineers, 2.4 percent technical support).[4] The functional employment of engineers is on average about the same in Japan and the United States, and among vehicle manufacturers and parts suppliers. In all cases slightly over 50 percent of the engineers are in product engineering, and the rest are in manufacturing. In addition, a small number of engineers may be assigned to marketing or to corporate planning staffs.

However, notwithstanding the averages, large differences can be observed within the industry in each country. In Japan, most of the differences can be attributed to the company's age and size (the smaller and younger the company, the higher share of engineers). In the U.S. in general, a higher ratio of engineering personnel may indicate a higher potential for new product development and improved process engineering. At the same time, the size of engineering overhead may negatively affect the competitive position individual firms. One could even argue that under some circumstances a lean engineering staff would give an advantage to the U.S. firms if the "savings" in the engineering manpower were not absorbed by a relative expansion in administrative personnel.

The disparity in the use of administrative personnel is most pronounced in the finance and accounting functions. In American company A the number of salaried employees in these two functions can be counted in the thousands, reaching 8 percent of total salaried employment; in company B the ratio is 10 percent. In contrast, in Japanese firm X this ratio is less than 2 percent, and the total number of financial staff is less than 500.

This is not to say that Japanese companies do not employ strict financial controls in their operations. However, the collection of financial data, as well as a substantial part of the financial analysis and planning, is delegated to line managers, and dual control systems are infrequent. The smaller size of Japanese automotive firms also plays a role. The resulting cash savings per car, considering only the salaries for the "surplus" financial staff, are over $120 in favor of the Japanese.

Another source of differences in administrative staffing between the two industries is the vertical organization of individual firms. Currently, a lot of attention is given in the U.S. automotive firms to streamlining the organizational hierarchy and reducing the layers of management. In most instances, such efforts usually result in a reduction of managerial layers in the factory, such as the elimination of general foreman or assistant plant managers. However, while such reductions are certainly useful in streamlining the organization, comparisons with Japanese manufacturers reveal that a top-heavy structure hampers effective communication and decisions from plant management upward rather than downward.

For example, in company A the Chief Executive Officer (CEO) is twelve to fourteen management layers away from a typical rank-and-file employee, and six or seven layers away from a typical plant manager. In company B the picture is similar. By contrast, plant managers in Japan are often appointed to the companies' Board of Directors and are at most only two reporting levels below the CEO.[5] Thus, the distance between the CEO and the rank-and-file is reduced, depending on the firm, to seven to nine layers.

The high status of Japanese plant managers is partly due to the fact that manufacturing sites in Japan are relatively larger (in number of employees) in comparison to the rest of the firm. Japanese vehicle manufacturers, while nominally much smaller in size than the U.S. firms, in fact represent mainly the assembly and engineering part of a much larger corporate group.[6] In that sense the propensity of Japanese firms to organize a family of independent firms—in a legal sense—rather than to build single-firm corporate empires allows them to reduce the levels of managers and free resources away from administration and control toward product and manufacturing development.

It seems that the U.S. manufacturers may have considerable room for improvement in the efficiency of management at the higher corporate levels. Part of the "surplus" of administrative personnel results from "demand" for staff to assist numerous senior managers and executives to coordinate activities on divisional and corporate levels. A typical Japanese Head Office department "in charge of affiliated companies" has only 20-30 employees, in contrast with the several thousands who engage in cross-divisional coordination in American firms.

In basic organizational units, such as divisions or plants, the main differences in structure among the U.S. and Japanese vehicle manufacturers is the span of control rather than the degree of vertical differentiation. Generally, Japanese executives and managers are assisted by several deputies, who while nominally second in authority are not in the direct line of supervision. Also, at the section level the span of control of a typical Japanese manager is substantially wider. For example, in the engineering area a Japanese engineering manager may supervise 10-15 employees as opposed to the 5-6 employees in American firms. As a result, an American Chief Engineer or Director may supervise three times less employees than his Japanese counterpart.[7]

It should be added that the composition of the white collar labor force is today in a state of flux due to personnel cutbacks or freezes implemented in both countries during the world recession of the past several years. In U.S. company A, while the number of white collar employees as a group declined in the same proportion as the number of blue collar workers, white collar employees assigned to sales decreased most, followed by technical support personnel, clericals, managers, and supervisors. However, the number of technical professionals remained stable. As a result, their share in the total white collar labor force increased by 10 percent. Similar changes were observed in company B, although in comparison to blue collar workers the decline for the white collar group was over 50 percent less.

In Japan the changing ratio of white collar labor is due to differences in the rates of labor force increase, as the increased competitive position of Japanese vehicle manufacturers protected their and their suppliers' employees from an employment decline. However, because of efforts to reduce the direct labor input through automation, the share of white collar employment since 1974 increased from 2 to 7 percent, depending on the firm. For example, in company Y direct labor decreased marginally, indirect labor increased by 2.9 percent annually, the number of administrators grew 4.1 percent annually, and the engineering professionals enjoyed the fastest growth: 4.7 percent per year.

Gender, Education, and Age Profiles

In both Japan and the U.S. the proportion of females in white collar jobs varies with occupational classification. For example, in American company A women workers comprise nearly 60 percent of office and clerical employees, but only 18 percent of technicians and professionals and 6.5 percent of managers. It should be pointed out that even though total employment in the U.S. automotive industry declined over the last several years, the proportion of women in technical and managerial jobs has increased. The same can be said about minority employment. In company A, 9.5 percent of managers and 10 percent of technicians and professionals are minority employees.

In Japanese firms, 24 to 25 percent of white collar employees are women, virtually all of them in nonmanagerial positions. Most of them are young office workers. For example, over 90 percent of women employed in company X are under 30. The vast majority of them still expect to retire when they marry or soon thereafter, and they are seldom assigned to jobs that may lead to future managerial positions. This lack of promotion opportunities reinforces their motivation to quit. Thus, in both countries, white collar employees in managerial or technical jobs are still predominantly male.

The educational profile of white collar employees in major Japanese and U.S. automotive firms is also similar (table 2). The proportion of employees with a college degree ranges from 33 to 38 percent. The number of employees with advanced degrees is still higher in the U.S. than in Japan, reflecting a traditionally higher reliance on formal training outside of the firm, as opposed to the on-the-job training practiced in Japan. This is true especially for administrative personnel; only a handful of MBA's work in the Japanese automotive industry. Among Japanese engineers, the proportion with graduate degrees has been on the rise since the mid-1970s.

Table 2
Education, Age, Seniority

	U.S.	Japan
% WC employees with college degree	33-38	36-42
% WC employees with advanced degree	6-10	5-7
% engineers with graduate degree	21-25	18-20
Average age of WC employees	41	37
% managers with 20+ years seniority	60-70	45-55

Among managers in American company B, about 50 percent have a college degree, and 20 percent an advanced degree. Among technical employees, 35 percent have bachelor degrees and 12 percent an advanced degree. In Japanese company X, only 3 percent of managers have advanced degrees, but 80 percent are college graduates. Among technical staff, nearly 60 percent have bachelor degrees and 11 percent have advanced degrees. Of those hired in the last 10 years, 78 percent have at least a college degree. In aggregate, about 19 percent of Japanese college-educated engineers have graduate degrees, compared to 23 percent for the U.S. vehicle manufacturers.

The average age of white collar employees is higher in the U.S. than in Japan: 41 in contrast to 33-34 (36-37 for male employees only). The same is true of parts suppliers in the two countries. Not surprisingly, given the well-known low interfirm mobility among large Japanese firms, the average tenure is high for all Japanese vehicle manufacturers. However, even longer tenure is characteristic of white collar employees in the U.S. auto industry. In company A only 5 percent of managers have less than 10 years of seniority, while 70 percent have been with the firm 20 years or longer. Only 14 percent are less than 40 years of age. Among engineers, 20 percent are less than 30, which is about equal to the proportion of those over 50 years old. In Japanese company Y, 30 percent of the engineering staff was hired during the last 10 years. Although the youngest manager is 35 years old, about 23 percent of managers are less than 40 years old.

Among managers in American car firms, over 80 percent have more than 20 years seniority with the firm, not much less than for Japanese vehicle manufacturers. It is interesting to note that among Japanese part suppliers the proportion of higher-level managers with seniority of less than 10 years is greater for the first-tier suppliers than among the second-tier firms: 47 versus 32 percent.[8] This can be explained by the fact that executive positions in first-tier suppliers are often staffed by retired officers from affiliated manufacturers. From the viewpoint of retiring managers, the second-tier suppliers offer generally much less attractive postretirement career opportunities.

Human Resource Management Functions

In American auto industry firms approximately 6-7 percent of white collar employees are assigned to the personnel/Industrial Relations (IR) area. In general, the number of personnel/IR staff has increased in the past decade partly in order to handle tasks associated with new federal and state regulations as well as to manage the expanded benefits. While the two functions are commonly split at the corporate staff level, they are often integrated on the division and plant levels. The link between the personnel/IR functions and the CEO varies by company, but it is usually less direct than in Japan.

White collar personnel control is mostly decentralized. For example, in company B the Head Office personnel staff of 170 people is responsible primarily for executive personnel control and general policy planning; personnel control of managers just below the executive level is the responsibility of the functional staff; the remaining managers or supervisors and other white collar employees are handled by division and plant personnel staffs. A typical divisional personnel office has approximately 25-35 employees, including a sizeable group administering benefits; personnel staff in plants vary in size from 5 to 40 depending on the size of the plant work force.

Japanese personnel staffs are relatively larger than in American firms. For example, in company X, 9.5 percent of all white collar employees are assigned to the personnel division or to personnel staff at the plant level. Nearly two-thirds of these work directly in one of the central personnel areas; the rest are guards, dormitory employees, and medical staff. The central personnel office has a staff of only 100 employees. It is responsible for personnel policies for both white collar and blue collar employees, although contract negotiations with the union are conducted through a specialized section. In a typical large manufacturing facility in

Japan (with approximately 4,000-5,000 workers), the personnel department is staffed on average with 60 personnel specialists. In addition, 15 dormitory employees, 15 employees maintaining recreation facilities, and 10 on the plant medical staff report to the head of the plant personnel.

The operational control of personnel is largely decentralized, as in the U.S. firms. However, the Japanese central personnel offices are more involved with the placement, appraisal, and promotions of all employees in managerial ranks. In the U.S. only the so-called "high-potential" managers are monitored by the central personnel staff. The Japanese personnel staff is also more involved in strategic planning activities. The amount of its strategic input closely matches that of other administrative functions, such as corporate planning, or finance. Consequently, in comparison to the Americans the Japanese personnel managers seem to enjoy higher prestige inside their organizations.

One of the main tasks of the corporate personnel function in both countries is the hiring and training of white collar employees. For a supply of employees with college education, companies in both countries rely on recruitment on college campuses. Exceptions exist (more frequently in the U.S. than in Japan), but the vast majority of college-educated employees are hired straight from school or a few years after graduation.[9] In the U.S. many white collar employees are hired from graduate schools, a trend which, as pointed out earlier, is also increasing in Japan, at least for engineering personnel.

College recruitment planning is in both countries coordinated by the central personnel staff. However, in Japan all college-educated employees are usually recruited through the Head Office and then assigned to divisions and plants; in the U.S. both direct and indirect placement is used. Also, in American firms there is no difference in the recruiting process for engineers and other college-educated employees. Although direct walk-ins do occur, most prospective employees sign up for an interview on their college campuses. After three or four rounds of interviews, final offers are made. In Japan administrative personnel are selected on the basis of applications solicited through mass mailings and promotion efforts on campuses, whereas engineers are selected using the university faculty or staff as an intermediary. In some instances, when demand exceeds supply, graduates may be oriented in their selection of companies. Such a mechanism assures most firms of a "fair share" and, at the same time, limits upward pressure on starting salaries.

So far there has been no general shortage of engineers in Japan, due mainly to past government efforts to expand the capacity of engineering departments. However, as the technological foundation of the automotive industry continues to change rapidly, many companies in the auto industry are facing the task of adapting to these changes by recruiting engineers with a particular technical knowledge. Those with electronic or information processing background are especially in high demand. For the future, in view of the fact that Japanese companies will be required to rely more than in the past on their own "in-house" R&D, demand for top-quality technical professionals is likely to increase. In order to respond to such a demand, a reform of the current university education system may be essential.

In the U.S. the need for reform may be more immediate as enrollment in engineering schools lags behind Japan and many other developed countries. Two factors are of concern here. First, teaching jobs in engineering colleges are unattractive relative to opportunities in the industry. Second, career opportunities in engineering fields seem limited in comparison to law, finance, or management consulting. For example, among firms in the automotive sector, the percentage of engineers on the companies' Board of Directors is 50 percent in Japan, but only 20 percent in the U.S.

To rectify this emerging imbalance, a joint effort of the U.S. corporate community and the public sector may be required since such educational issues are beyond the control of any single company. However, in order to promote such an effort, a better plan for developing engineering and technical manpower is desirable. Such planning for the future is only beginning to be implemented in U.S. firms as it is in Japan.

White collar employees in both countries can take advantage of large training programs sponsored by their employers. The U.S. firms rely to a greater extent on courses and training offered by outside institutions, mostly nearby universities and colleges. With a few exceptions, such as Senior Manager Development Programs at leading business schools, program, course, or seminar selection is typically left to the employee's initiative. For college courses there are only very broad limits in terms of tuition refund policies. In Japan, in contrast, the emphasis is on internal training programs. Developmental planning is more structured, and course or program selection results from discussions between the employee and his/her manager and is monitored by the personnel staff. On-the-job training in Japanese firms is limited to lower-level white collar employees.

High-potential employees in both countries are often rotated through special developmental assignments. International assignments and cross-functional and cross-divisional moves are especially desirable. However, for the white collar employees as a group, those in Japan have more opportunities to move for training purposes, although there is not much difference in overall job mobility. For example, in American company B and Japanese company X, a significant difference in the overall volume of job mobility within the two firms was observed only for managers with a technical background. For managers in nontechnical jobs, no significant difference in frequency of job changes was detected.[10]

In both countries the cross-functional job mobility of nontechnical managers is higher than the mobility of engineers. In other words, engineers have a less general career experience than nonengineers. The comparisons also indicate that differences in cross-functional mobility patterns are larger between occupational classes (e.g., engineers vs. nonengineers) than between countries. Therefore, it seems that the popular perception that contrasts the Japanese "generalist" manager with the American "specialist" manager may at best be an oversimplification.[11]

Where American and Japanese managers differ most is in the amount of interdivisional mobility. Japanese managers, nonengineers even more than those with technical backgrounds, rotate through many parts of the organization (though often within the same function). This contributes to their effective socialization into the firm, improves communication and control, and reduces the cost of control and supervision. As a result, the job rotation system of Japanese automotive firms has a direct positive impact on their ability to facilitate flexibility, innovation, and organizational change.

Also, in the performance appraisal process some differences between the two countries can be observed. In American automotive firms, appraisal of white collar employees is generally linked to an employee's potential. Management appraisals are coordinated by the central staff, but only higher-level managers and executives are reviewed by the Executive Office. Others are reviewed in divisions and plants. The process is annual and requires five months from the drafting of guidelines until the final review. The appraisal at all levels is designed to be performance oriented. Recently, in several firms an evaluation of management style was also added into the appraisal in order to stimulate participative management. Succession planning is an integrated part of the appraisal process, and promotions are seldom granted unless an appropriate position in the upper rank is available.

In Japanese firms the appraisal system differs on several basic characteristics. First, the cohort of peers with similar education, seniority, and status forms the base for performance comparisons. Second, the evaluation process is centralized, and the performance of all managerial-class employees is reviewed in the central personnel office. Third, an employee's performance is reviewed more often, generally at least two or three times a year, in conjunction with bonus payments in summer and winter and with salary and status reviews in spring or in autumn. Finally, while self-report and interview with an employee are key components of the evaluation system, the decision as to whether to inform him of the appraisal results is usually left to the discretion of his or her immediate superior.

In this respect it is interesting to note the impact of the characterization of the evaluation process on the distribution of managers within a firm. In the Japanese firms, managers ranked low tend to be concentrated in divisions and departments peripheral to the main-line business. In contrast, in the U.S. firms the proportion of managers with low rankings is higher in large core divisions relative to the company as a whole. This, however, inhibits the company's ability to leverage the size of a business unit with delegation of authority and increased autonomy for middle managers.

Compensation System

Direct comparisons of compensation of white collar employees in American and Japanese automotive firms are complicated by a number of factors, such as the cash value of benefits, or bonus eligibility. However, at least partial comparisons are feasible if the focus of inquiry is limited to cash compensation payable to a majority of white collar employees. In Japan that would include the bonus that is payable to all employees basically in proportion to their salaries.[12] In the U.S. the bonus is excluded from the base compensation since over 80 percent of white collar employees are not eligible for supplementary compensation plans. Three questions are of interest here: the patterns of cash compensation in firms within each country, the absolute levels of compensation, and differences in compensation levels between white and blue collar employees.

At the entry level the starting salaries in the U.S. are generally substantially higher than those in Japan. For example, for college-educated engineers, starting salaries in large American automotive companies range between $22,000-27,000, for parts suppliers, between $20,000-28,000. In Japan, starting salaries for engineers range from $9,500 to $10,500. Each year thereafter an employee is awarded a pay raise equal to an average increase for his age group plus or minus his merit rating. The base wage for senior employees may reach 250-300 percent of the starting salaries, but the seniority wage curve begins to taper off in the second decade of employment and becomes virtually flat for employees with 20 or more years of tenure. Additional increases are awarded on merit only. The pay differentials based on performance are relatively small, but in the absence of attractive job opportunities outside of the firm, they are sufficient to foster intense competition. Seniority is a necessary, but not a sufficient, condition of success.

In both countries white collar entry salaries are 15 to 25 percent above the entry wages for blue collar personnel. However, as a consequence of the seniority wage system established in Japanese firms, annual wage increases granted to blue collar workers follow the pattern set up for white collar employees (in fact, the basic wage structure is the same for both groups). In the U.S. blue collar wages do not change after the first 18 months of employment (except by across-the-board contractual increase, or by reassignment to a skill-trade job). A more detailed scheme of the two systems can be illustrated in the example of a cohort of white collar employees with 20 years of seniority in American firm A, and in Japanese firm J (figure 1).

In the U.S. case the reward system is structured along salary grades and ranks. Just over 50 percent of the cohort is in rank A (plant superintendants, marketing managers, supervisors in product engineering) with an estimated cohort average salary of $43,000; 30 percent are in rank B (estimated average salary $54,000); 15 percent in rank C (estimated average salary $76,000); and 3 percent in rank D, which also includes all executive positions (estimated cohort average $111,000). The average cohort salary is about $54,000, nearly 30 percent above the Japanese cohort average of $42,500.

However, in contrast to the relatively broad interrank salary differentials in the U.S. firm, the highest paid Japanese employees receive only $2,500 above their cohort average (table 3), and less than 10 percent of employees receive less than $40,000. In other words, the average compensation for Japanese employees is equal to the compensation for the bottom 50 percent of the U.S. employees with the same seniority. At the same time it is notable that salary compression is less of an issue in Japan than in the U.S. It may be that the negative motivational impact of salary compression at the lower levels of American organizational hierarchies is accentuated by wide interrank differentials. In Japan both intrarank and interrank differentials are compressed, thus lowering employees' expectations.

Table 3
Compensation Ratios

	U.S.	Japan
Top WC/Average WC*	200/100	106/100
Average WC/Average BC*	220/100	140/100
Top WC/Top BC*	500/100	150/100
CEO/Top BC	1500/100	700/100

*employees with 20 years of experience

Finally, an "average" U.S. white collar employee with 20 years of seniority receives nearly 120 percent more in annual cash compensation than a blue collar coworker of similar age; for top performers among the white collar group, the difference increases up to 500 percent. In Japan the difference is less than 40 percent considering the average compensation levels for the two groups, and only marginally higher for the elite. Thus, the income differential between the two groups of employees is, on average, nearly three times as large in the U.S. firm, nearly eight times as large in the case of the elite. This is a conservative estimate, not including the bonus payable to the high-ranking American employees.

Similar trends become apparent when the salaries of key executives of the vehicle manufacturers in the two countries are considered. The average salary of a Japanese CEO, including bonus, is generally not more than 6-8 times higher than the income of the highest-paid blue collar employee. For the U.S., even if bonus and stock options are excluded, such a ratio is in the 12-18 range, again more than double the income differentials observed in Japan. However, in profitable years when American executives collect bonuses and stock options, this difference may triple, as happened in 1983.

Two explanations can be suggested for this phenomenon. On the one hand, the lower income differentiation in Japan can be attributed to the deliberate policy of maintaining the cohesiveness of the organization by reducing salary differences across different strata of employees. On the other hand, it can be argued that such a policy can be effective only when the dominance of Internal Labor Markets in the economy restricts the mobility of movement across different companies or industries, especially for high-ranking managers and executives.

Again, with respect to noncash benefits, direct comparisons are difficult due to differences in accounting procedures (e.g., retirement payments).[13] However, it can be estimated from the available data that in both countries retirement, health care, insurance, and other welfare benefits average between an additional 20 to 30 percent of white collar compensation, not counting social security taxes payable by the employers. Japanese manufacturers enjoy a clear advantage in the area of medical benefits. By combining national health insurance and company-operated medical clinics and hospitals, their medical costs are running at 20 percent of what U.S. companies have to pay. On the other hand, a number of benefits common in Japan are not costed out in wage/benefit statistics, the most important being housing mortgage subsidies, recreation complexes, etc.

The differences in compensation rates in the two countries have serious consequences for the competitiveness of the American automobile industry. An analysis conducted by Flynn,[14] based on data presented in this article and on an earlier work of Abernathy, Harbour and Henn,[15] led to the conclusion that at current exchange rates the white collar compensation costs contribute about 48 percent of the total labor cost difference. Even if the American firms matched Japanese productivity and eliminated the blue collar wage differential, the total labor cost differential would still remain close to $1,000 per car.

Future Trends and Policy Implications

Although future growth may vary by company, the maturation of the auto markets will limit opportunities for growth for the industry as a whole, and, by extension, opportunity for employee advancement may be restricted as well. If unchecked, this may result in a decline in motivation among white collar employees and a loss of the talent necesary for these enterprises to other, still-growing industries. The motivational "technology" may become an important strategic resource. Under the circumstances outlined above, the centrality of the Human Resource function to competitive strategy will increase dramatically.

In order to reduce the white collar overhead cost to a level that would make the U.S. industry competitive with Japan, significant changes in the Human Resources systems currently in place in the industry will be necessary. In particular, the internal organization at the executive level has to be streamlined well beyond present efforts (such as the current GM reorganization), both to reduce cost and to improve communication. The U.S. firms are simply too big, too fat, and too slow to respond effectively to the deepening internationalization of the industry, to the vast changes in manufacturer-supplier relations, and to the ever increasing need for productivity improvements on and off the production line.

In addition, the auto industries in both countries will have to adjust their Human Resource Management systems to the profound organizational changes stemming from the accelerated introduction of new technology. For example, the computerization of design (CAD/CAM) in the product engineering area, the automation and robotization of manufacturing processes in the process engineering area, and office automation in administration will necessitate changes in the employment structure of white collar employees, as well as require a massive retraining if the present employees are to qualify for new jobs.

To face this challenge, the auto manufacturers in both countries have to continue refocusing their Human Resource Management strategies concerning white collar employees to respond to the changes in the environment. The target of these strategies is clear and well understood: to enhance flexible and timely adaptation to technological change, encourage innovation, and most generally, mobilize the creative potential of all. The ability to implement these objectives will determine the winners.

NOTES

[1]The data presented in this article were collected under the auspices of the Joint U.S.-Japan Automotive Study, The Center for Japanese Studies, The University of Michigan, and Technova Inc., Tokyo. For the report of this study, see Robert E. Cole and Taizo

Yakushiji, eds., *The American and Japanese Auto Industries in Transition* (Ann Arbor, MI and Tokyo: The Center for Japanese Studies, The University of Michigan, and Technova, Inc., 1984).

This article is reprinted from the *Columbia Journal of World Business*, Fall 1984, pp. 87-94. Used by permission of the publisher.

[2]For example, see Daniel Roos and Alan Altshuler, codirectors, *The Future of the Automobile* (Cambridge, MA: The MIT Press, 1984), and William J. Abernathy, Kim B. Clark, and Alan M. Kantrow, *Industrial Renaissance: Producing a Competitive Future for America* (New York: Basic Books, 1983), chapters 5 and 7.

[3]Within the scope of this article, white collar employees are defined as managers, supervisors, administrators, technical professionals and support personnel, sales employees, and clerical workers.

[4]In absolute numbers, however, over 50 percent more engineering and technical personnel are employed by the U.S.-based vehicle manufacturers, whose total employment is some 700,000 compared to 215,000 for the nine auto-producers in Japan. For details see Lawrence T. Harbeck, "Technical Manpower Characteristics of the U.S. and Japanese Automotive Industry," Research Report (Ann Arbor, MI: Joint U.S.-Japan Automotive Study, 1983).

[5]In Nissan, four out of eight key manufacturing sites are headed by Corporate Directors. In Honda, four key sites are headed by members of the Board of Directors, including one Managing Director.

[6]Both Toyota and Nissan control over 20 affiliated firms that engage in a number of business activities from components manufacturing and subassembly to insurance and transportation services. For details see Dodwell & Co., *Industrial Groupings in Japan* (Tokyo: Dodwell Marketing Consultants, 1980).

[7]Lawrence T. Harbeck, op. cit.

[8]Fumio Kodama, Taizo Yakushiji, and Mieko Hanaeda, "Structural Characteristics of the Japanese Automotive Supplier Industry," Joint U.S.-Japan Automotive Study, Working Paper 13 (Ann Arbor, MI: The Center for Japanese Studies, The University of Michigan, 1983).

[9]Until very recently, many college-educated employees of General Motors were graduates of the GM-sponsored "General Motors Institute." Direct institutional sponsorship was, however, recently discontinued.

[10]Vladimir Pucik, J. Imai-Marquez, and M. L. Wolford, "Management Career Patterns in the U.S. and Japanese Auto

Industry," in R. Cole, ed., *The U.S. and Japanese Auto Industries: Point and Counterpoint*, forthcoming.

[11]Such contrasts were made, for example, by W. G. Ouchi (*Theory Z* [Reading, MA: Addison-Wesley, 1981]); N. Suzuki (*Management and Industrial Structure in Japan* [New York: Pergamon Press, 1981]); and Ezra F. Vogel (*Japan as Number One* [Cambridge, MA: Harvard University Press, 1981]).

[12]For discussion of the Japanese bonus and benefit systems see Michael S. Flynn, "Compensation Levels and Systems: Implications for Organizational Competitiveness in the U.S. and Japanese Automotive Industries," Joint U.S.-Japan Automotive Study, Working Paper 20 (Ann Arbor, MI: The Center for Japanese Studies, The University of Michigan, 1984).

[13]See Michael S. Flynn, "Estimating Comparative Compensation Costs and Their Contribution to the Manufacturing Cost Difference," Joint U.S.-Japan Automotive Study, Working Paper 21 (Ann Arbor, MI: The Center for Japanese Studies, The University of Michigan, 1984), part 3.

[14]Michael S. Flynn, op. cit.

[15]William J. Abernathy, J. E. Harbour, and I. M. Henn, "Productivity and Comparative Cost Advantages: Some Estimates for Major Automotive Producers," Harvard Business School Working Paper, 1981.

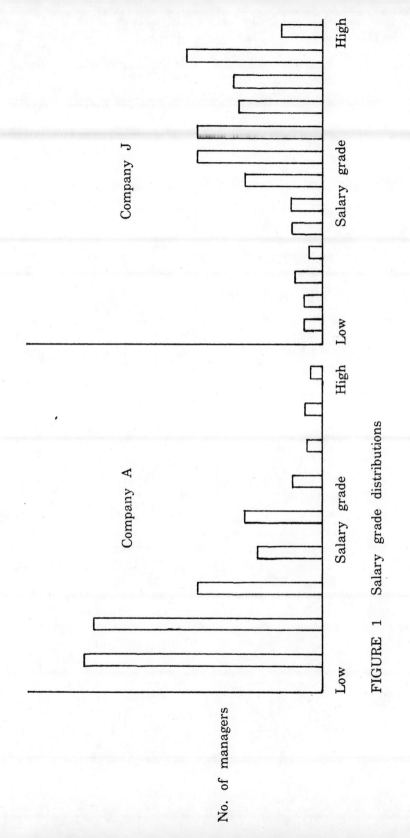

No. of managers

Company A

Company J

Low   Salary grade   High

Low   Salary grade   High

Salary grade distributions

FIGURE 1

The Internationalization of the
Automobile Industry*

Daniel T. Jones

Introduction

This paper presents some of the results of the recently completed MIT Future of the Automobile Program (Roos and Altshuler 1984). It outlines the major forces that are shaping the worldwide automobile industry and presents our conclusions on the changing location of production and structure of the industry. It concludes by situating the European industry in the changing global context and assessing its strengths and weaknesses throughout the 1980s.

Three Transformations in the History of the Industry

Our primary interest is in trying to evaluate and interpret the impact of the many factors that are beginning to change the nature of competition in this industry and, hence, its structure, ownership, and location in the 1980s and 1990s. The underlying idea is that present developments in this industry and the relative strengths and weaknesses of the main participants can be best understood, on the one hand, through an analysis of the major technological and/or managerial breakthroughs that have transformed this industry over time and, on the other, through a systematic evaluation of how these have diffused throughout the rest of the industry. These must of course be related to the prevailing international economic situation and to government policies influencing international trade, foreign investment flows, etc.

113

In our analysis of the history of this industry, we identify three major transformations that have shaped it. Each of these arose from a creative breakthrough by a particular set of producers in technology and/or the organization of the industry, which facilitated a rapid growth of demand and led to a powerful export threat to producers in the rest of the world. The first of these transformations, occurring around 1910, was the change by American producers from custom building to mass production. The second occurred in Western Europe in the late 1950s, when European producers combined mass production with an emphasis on product innovation or differentiation to challenge American-based production for the first time. The third commenced in Japan in the late 1960s, when Japanese producers made dramatic breakthroughs in production organization that soon yielded a lower-cost product of far greater manufacturing accuracy.

The consequence of each transformation was that a new region of the world seized the initiative in shaping the future of the industry worldwide. At the same time, the remaining producers embarked on a process of catching up as the new best practice was diffused to other producers, often in association with strong government mediation to stem the trade imbalances resulting from the breakthrough and, hence, the superior competitiveness of those producers.

Abernathy describes the confluence of product and process innovations that were combined by Henry Ford in a unique way to create the mass-production automobile and the flow-line production system (Abernathy 1978). These were combined with a number of social and organizational innovations, such as the introduction of the eight-hour day, much higher wages, and a thorough application of the scientific management principles of Taylor and others in segmenting the work process and routinizing work tasks. This division of labor of the work process was later extended by Alfred Sloan in General Motors, who added a highly differentiated management pyramid on top of the basic shop-floor organization of Ford (Sloan 1972). In this way, management functions were differentiated and refined, leading in the marketing area, for instance, to a wider range of product offerings to cater to different market segments and annual styling changes. All of these organizational innovations, when combined, represented an essential breakthrough that enabled the development of such a complex mass-production industry.

The results of these developments were a rapid growth of production to 5.4 million units in 1929, a concentration of production in the hands of three producers, and a flow of exports to Western Europe (see table 1 and figure 1). Abernathy describes how, after the initial breakthroughs, the development of the U.S. industry settled down to an even more increased refinement of the original concepts, right up until it was challenged in the mid-1970s.

Table 1
World Auto Production and Exports, 1929-1980
(million units)

	1929	1938	1950	1960	1970	1980
World Auto Prod.						
North America	4.8	2.1	7.0	7.0	7.5	7.2
Western Europe	0.6	0.9	1.1	5.1	10.4	10.4
Japan				0.2	3.2	7.0
Centrally Planned		0.1	0.1	0.3	0.7	2.1
Rest of world				0.4	1.0	1.8
Total	*5.4*	*3.1*	*8.2*	*13.0*	*22.8*	*28.6*
World Auto Exp.						
intra N. America	0.1				0.9	1.1
from N. America	0.4	0.2	0.1	0.1	0.1	0.1
intra W. Europe		0.1	0.2	1.0	2.7	3.7
from W. Europe	0.1	0.1	0.4	1.2	1.8	1.3
Japan					0.7	3.9
Other					0.2	0.8
Total	*0.6*	*0.4*	*0.7*	*2.3*	*6.4*	*10.9*
Exp. as % prod.	11%	13%	9%	18%	28%	38%

Sources: SMMT, MVMA, L'Argus, Automotive News, JAMA, Comecon Yearbooks.

The European response was to mediate the trade flows resulting from the competitive imbalance with the U.S. by erecting trade barriers. The U.S. producers in turn responded by building modern plants in European countries, where they were allowed to. European producers incorporated what they had learned from visiting Detroit, but the full benefits of scientific management and mass-production technology had to await the opening up of the European market in the postwar period.

When the European recovery took place after World War II, the automobile industry grew rapidly. However, circumstances in each country were quite different, leading to different kinds of products being built in those countries. These differences have largely persisted to the present day, where producers in each country have accumulated quite different technical, design, and styling expertise. The opening up of the European market created a very substantial inter-European trade in complementary products and led to European producers taking over the dominance of world automobile trade for the first twenty-five years after World War II (see table 1 and figure 1.) While the opening up of the European market was necessary to exploit the benefits of the scale economies offered by production and organizational techniques developed in the U.S., the diversity of European producers, contrary to the conventional wisdom of "The American Challenge" of the 1960s, was to become its greatest strength (Schreiber 1969). As American firms tapped the European market, some European firms mounted a powerful challenge to the U.S. industry in the small-car segment previously ignored by the U.S. producers.

There were many calls in the U.S. for government mediation to stop this flow of cars from Europe. These were forestalled by the general buoyancy of the world economy, the devaluation of the dollar in 1971 just as European wages were rising—which transformed a trade flow into a flow of investment as Volkswagen opened its first plant in the U.S.—and the arrival of the first U.S.-produced small cars. The diversity of the European producers was their strength. When the Japanese captured the small-car market in the U.S. in the 1970s, some of the European producers went up-market and created an entirely new, high-priced luxury segment. Currently, almost all the 200,000 cars sold per year in the U.S. priced over $20,000 come from West Germany, Sweden, or the U.K. This helps to boost the profitability of those producers, particularly as the dollar strengthens against the European currencies.

Government policy was instrumental in prioritizing the automobile industry for development in Japan after World War II, and the industry grew up under the protection of high tariffs and the prohibition of foreign ownership. During this development the Japanese brought in both the best management practices from the U.S. and the latest product technology under license from Europe.

By adapting these management ideas to Japanese priorities, such as limited space, materials, and energy, and building on the ability of the Japanese to work together in groups, they arrived at a unique synthesis of the "just-in-time" production system combined with "total quality control." As this system was refined, a much cheaper product of much higher quality was created. The competitive advantage was reinforced by a shift to smaller cars in the U.S. following the 1973 and, especially, 1979 oil crises. The Japanese quickly came to dominate world trade by 1980 (see both table 1 and figure 1).

By 1981 this had led to some form of formal or informal arrangement to restrain or control Japanese imports in all the major car-producing nations of North America and Western Europe. Since then the Japanese producers have begun to establish production operations or joint ventures in a number of countries, including the U.S., Canada, Italy, and Spain. The four major Japanese producers have announced plans to produce up to one million cars a year in North America by 1988. Meanwhile, European and American producers are beginning to adopt many of the advances pioneered by the Japanese, either through direct copying of what they have seen in Japan, through collaboration with the Japanese (as BL is doing with Honda for instance), or by observing the activities of Japanese-owned plants in their own countries. Early results suggest that much of the Japanese management paradigm is transferable to the West, and direct foreign investment by the Japanese will have a powerful demonstration effect in breaking down resistance from both middle management and the work force.

Japanese Management: A Third Transformation

There is no doubt that the Japanese have made a major leap forward in the art of organizing automobile production. Their ultimate goal was to develop a continuous flow from the sheet steel or roll and foundry to customer delivery, without any intermediate buffers or inventory, and to integrate the supply of components from outside firms into the production process. The full adoption of the *kanban*, or "just-in-time" system, depends in part on having component suppliers located nearby, but more importantly on overturning a number of basic assumptions held by production engineers in the West. In Europe and the U.S., buffer stocks and inventories are held because of the slowness in tooling changes, fear of equipment breakdown, supplier nondelivery, or other disruptions to the system. In Japan, the absence of buffers and the fact that the whole production system depends on the bottlenecks being highlighted and tackled quickly has led them to fine tune the system to a high degree. Such a system also depends on a zero defects policy, where the elimination of defects also eliminates problems at the next stage and the need for expensive off-line rectification. This contrasts with the commonly held assumption that to eliminate the last percentage of defects raises costs and slows down production. Quite the reverse is true when one gets rid of independent inspectors, expensive test facilities, and the man-hours spent in fault rectification.

In addition to the advances in production organization within the plant, Japanese car firms have developed a quite unique set of relationships with their suppliers that overcomes many of the weaknesses of vertically integrated companies in the West and arms-length relations with independent suppliers. The cross ownership links between Japanese car firms (not majority shareholdings) and their suppliers are built around the coordination of strategy, cooperation in R&D and product development, and tight production scheduling. Suppliers remain independent economic units so full costs are known, unlike many traditionally vertically integrated companies. Relationships are, by definition, long-term, emphasizing the maximum flow of information and the rapid diffusion of new managerial practices and new technologies such as computer-aided design (CAD).

Membership of the large Keiretsu groups, such as the Mitsubishi, Sumitomo, and Mitsui groups, also confers very important advantages to Japanese car firms in relation to financing, labor-force flexibility, and access to other areas of technology in other group companies (such as electronics). Competition between these Keiretsu groups across a whole range of industries is strategic in nature, and no group has been willing to exit an important industrial sector. Therefore, competition between these groups is extremely intense and, because of the inability to force a competitor to exit, focuses on long-term market share, quality, and efficiency. This intense competition within Japan spills over into export markets and has not led to the concentration of production in the hands of a few companies as has happened everywhere else. When combined, the advances in in-plant organization, relations with suppliers, and the industrial group organization in Japan represent a completely new management paradigm significantly different from the scientific management of mass production developed by Ford, Sloan, and others.

A considerable literature now exists on the Japanese approach to mass-production organization, and a number of studies have reported on detailed aspects of the system (see Schonberger 1982; Clark 1979; Magaziner and Hout 1980; Dodwell & Co. 1980; and White and Trevor 1983). Even after installation of the most modern equipment, considerable knowledge has to be gained before the same degree of fine tuning that the Japanese reached in the last decade can be achieved. In the meantime, the Japanese are not standing still.

Electronics and New Materials: A Fourth Transformation

While still coping with the dramatic consequences of the third transformation, the automobile industry is also well into a fourth transformation. After a long gestation period in the aircraft and computer industries, microelectronics are creating new possibilities in the automobile industry.

There is no doubt that, in contrast to the last twenty years, there are a whole range of new technologies that are being incorporated into new designs of automobiles. As a result of a significant investment in R&D over the last decade by the automobile industry and the advent of a range of advances in electronics and materials technologies, there is a broader and growing shelf of new technological alternatives currently available to the automobile designer (Seiffert and Walzer 1984). Although these new technologies will be incorporated step by step over the next decade or so, the result will be that the car of the early 1990s will differ completely in almost every respect from the car of the early 1980s. In a period of rapid technological evolution in every part of the automobile, it is impossible to predict what the winning combination of all these developments will be. Therefore, the scope for many different producers to pick off unique combinations of new technologies and to create quite distinctive cars is enormous. There is, moreover, no reason to think that all the cards are in the hands of the very large producers with huge resources at their disposal. In the past many important advances have been introduced by small- and medium-sized producers. This will continue to be the case. The product is not mature and is unlikely to become so in the foreseeable future.

In addition to a major change in the pace of technological advancement in the product, a similar revolution is taking place in major items of production tooling. Until recently the trend in production technology was toward ever more dedicated automated lines for producing bodies or machining engines. These lines were geared to high-volume continuous output of a standardized product. They were not flexible, and the tooling had to be completely replaced for a new model or engine (see Abernathy 1978). In the late 1970s the advent of computer-controlled production lines and the introduction of more flexible automation involving robots, automated handling, machining cells, etc. have changed the economies of scale in production dramatically. The use of robots instead of dedicated multiwelders, for instance, gives those plants a greater degree of flexibility to switch models in response to demand and reduces the cost of introducing new models and variants. A similar degree of flexibility has also been incorporated into new automated stamping lines, allowing rapid die changes so press runs can be shorter, saving considerably on inventory costs. Having substantially transformed the stamping, welding, painting, and machining operations, flexible automation is now spreading to the trim shop and the assembly of components, subassemblies, and final assembly. Volkswagen claims that 25 percent of the final assembly of the new Golf is now automated, with engine, brake linings, batteries, and wheels fitted automatically. Austin Rover is now automatically fitting windscreens in their new Montego. All of this assembly automation is also readily reprogrammable for new models and variants.

This flexibility is extremely important if models have to be changed more frequently to keep pace with the rapidly changing state of the art. A flexible line of robots can be replaced piecemeal as new generations of robots become available. Robot lines give greater scope for refining the production layout and organization since the learning process with this equipment allows one to fine tune the production process along Japanese lines, particularly as production control becomes more automated.

A more modular approach to production also allows the addition of subsequent production modules, rather than the more expensive commitment to a completely dedicated line for maximum anticipated volume. Although the initial cost of switching from dedicated to flexible automation is high, the subsequent investment in designing and introducing new models and variants will probably be lower than in the past. Likewise, the cost of updating production tooling step by step with new technology will be substantially lower than with dedicated systems once the initial switch has been made. The growing use of high-tensile steel, aluminum, and plastic parts have already reduced the number of welds required. Further advances by the end of the decade may dramatically change the techniques of production.

Diffusion of new flexible automation has been very rapid since the late 1970s, and by the mid-1980s almost all the major production facilities in Europe, Japan, and the U.S. will have been substantially retooled in this way. A second wave of plant retooling is now occurring in the components industry. The major consequence of these advances in production technology has been to reduce the economies of scale in production, thereby reducing the pressure for a minimum output of two million units. A full range of cars can now be produced in one or two plants at a much lower total volume and at a cost competitive with much larger producers. There is no doubt that this has been the biggest factor to change the fortunes of small- and medium-sized producers. Smaller producers such as Saab and Austin Rover are pioneering the development of smaller-scale production tooling, which will not be such a high priority for larger producers like General Motors, Ford, and Volkswagen. These new, flexible production techniques are therefore opening up a much wider choice of production possibilities at quite different production volumes in contrast to the convergence in techniques and scale economies with dedicated production automation. Moreover, we have only begun to see the changes in production technology; more are in prospect. Economies of scale are also changing in the design activity through the advent of CAD, CAE, and CAM. The production tooling is therefore also not mature, and economies of scale will not be as important a driving force as they have been in the past.

Developments in the Market

Most analyses of the evolution of demand by observers outside the automobile producers themselves have concentrated on the overall level of demand and have not investigated changes in the pattern of demand in different market segments. When this is done, it becomes obvious that the product is not commoditylike, and that demand in different market segments and countries has behaved quite differently over time.

While it is true that the anticipated growth of the market in all the major OECD countries will be much lower than in the past, and that a high proportion of it will be for replacement purposes, the

composition of this demand is not at all mature, and patterns of
demand are not converging between countries (see OECD 1984 for
recent forecasts of overall volume levels).

Figure 2 shows the pattern of demand in the main markets
for 1973 and 1982 and reveals that apart from the big shift to
smaller cars in the U.S., the pattern of demand was relatively stable
in the other countries. Figure 2 also shows that the patterns of
demand in each of these markets are and have remained quite
different from each other. National producers who rely heavily on
their domestic market for a large proportion of their sales have
concentrated on producing the types of cars most in demand in their
home markets and have often found great difficulties in developing
the skills and expertise to compete in quite different market
segments. For instance, Fiat and Renault, with their expertise in
small cars, have never developed a successful presence in the
large-car market. Producers moving to completely new market
segments typically require three product generations to catch up
with the leaders in that segment. This has been true of the Japanese
producers moving up-market into larger cars and the U.S. producers
moving down to smaller cars. General Motors concedes that it will be
the late 1980s before they can produce their own small car
competitively in the U.S., a decade after the 1979 oil shock.

In addition to the lack of convergence in patterns of demand
between countries, we observe a considerable change in the way the
market is segmented. In the past there was a simple correlation
between large size and luxury and small size and utility. Now the
segmentation looks more like a matrix, with luxury, sporty, family,
and utility cars in each size class. Some producers, notably the
Japanese, are coming out with new packages that define completely
new segments of the market. The Honda Accord set new standards
of small-car luxury in the U.S., and the Nissan Prairie introduces a
new class of utility vehicle. We are therefore witnessing a divergence
in the types of cars being demanded rather than a convergence on a
few basic and increasingly similar "world car" designs. Certainly,
we are seeing some models manufactured in different locations, like
the Volkswagen Golf and the Renault 9 and 11. However, the trend
is toward extracting the maximum number of quite different
variants from a common set of body and mechanical components.
The Escort and Cavalier were completely redesigned for the U.S.
market, sharing almost no common components with their European
counterparts, hence throwing away any potential savings in design
and production costs.

We also observe that while domestic producers have specialized in the dominant size of car demanded in their home market, imports by foreign-based producers have been least in those segments (see figure 3). This means that foreign-based producers have essentially built up their export business on the basis of their strength in a particular market segment (e.g., Renault and Fiat in small cars) while selling a limited number of the rest of their range on the back of these. Most of the volume producers have a large share of their domestic market but only a 3 to 5 percent share of the other markets in Europe. This residual share of the other markets is in part because the foreign producer offers a better product in a market segment in which the domestic producer is not as strong and because there are always some customers who want something different with a clearly identifiable distinguishing characteristic from the popular domestic brand (such as a firm, solidly built German car or a comfortably riding and idiosyncratic French car). As soon as producers try to move away from their national characteristics, they stand to lose this market share in other countries. These observations of course hold for the major producing markets and not the smaller open markets with no domestic production. The former, however, account for the major part of demand in the developed world.

All these observations lead one to the conclusion that there is great potential for all kinds of product differentiation, and few producers will want to risk laying down very large capacity for one model, as General Motors did with the X car in the U.S. Instead, we are going to see a greater proliferation of models and variants in the second half of the 1980s and more deliberate emphasis on a unique image and on the national characteristics of each vehicle producer. The difficulties Volkswagen faced in the U.S. in selling a U.S.-built car are a case in point. As the market becomes more fragmented, the potential for skillfully seeking out market niches and creating a particular image is enhanced. Our observation is also that small- and medium-sized producers are currently more adept at making such moves and seeking out market niches. This is exemplified by the European specialist producers—Volvo, Saab, Daimler Benz, BMW, Jaguar—and by Chrysler in the U.S. and Honda and Mazda in Japan.

Dematurity and the Future Structure of the Industry

The above analysis shows that in contrast to the conventional view outlined, all the major elements of competitiveness in this industry are in a state of great flux and change; the markets, the product, the production equipment, and the way the industry is managed are all no longer mature. Moreover, this dematurity presents great new opportunities for specialist and medium-sized producers. We foresee no stable global oligopoly emerging in the next decade or two, nor do we see a great shift of production out of the developed economies as a result of this dematurity. Many of the theoretical advantages of low-cost production in the newly industrializing countries were in any case offset by much lower productivity, a lower degree of system efficiency, higher component costs, and acute macroeconomic, fiscal, and exchange-rate uncertainties in those countries.

In the period of dematurity over the next two decades, we conclude that most of the existing automobile producers will probably survive in some form. We do not envisage many new entrants, however, because the accumulation of experience and skills in combining complex systems into a harmonious package is difficult to acquire, the initial investment required is high, and the risk of failure is great. The only likely route would be through a supplier of radical new component technology that moves up into final assembly when its new technology redefines the product or production system to such an extent that it provides a competitive opening. The move from systems supplier to assembler is, however, very difficult. Moreover, we do not foresee the kind of radical one-step technological development (such as an electric car competitive with existing products) being produced in substantial volume in the next decade.

Although we envisage most of the existing medium-sized producers surviving this decade, this survival will be precarious and testing, and they are still under various constraints. In particular, medium-sized producers are not in a position to finance all the activities that a larger producer can. A medium-sized producer therefore has to identify both its particular strengths and the capabilities that must be retained in order to remain an independent automobile producer. The answer to these constraints lies in a mixture of buying major components, jointly developing and procuring others, cooperatively designing with other producers, and substantially relying on the acquisition of technical knowledge from others. In other words, one has to trade in one's weak areas. To do so successfully depends on retaining a strong engineering capability in order to make the correct technical choices in purchasing decisions, to skillfully combine the different inputs, and to be able to absorb the technology acquired from others. The key to survival is flexible management with good internal communication, combined with a strong technical base.

A similar pattern of cooperation is also emerging between the larger producers, with a host of joint ventures in engines, transmissions, and new models in recent years, as well as an increasing cross trade between manufacturers in major components, including engines and even license production ventures. In addition, one is beginning to see wider forms of cooperation involving whole areas of strengths and weaknesses, such as the provision of manufacturing know-how in return for market access and/or a broadened distribution system. An example of this is the General Motors-Toyota joint venture in Fremont, California. Toyota wants to gain experience in manufacturing under American conditions while gaining a broader access to the U.S. market. General Motors wants a demonstration plant for new manufacturing techniques, manning levels, and products in small-market segments while it works on new small-car designs of its own for the late 1980s. These patterns of cooperation in the short run in the context of competition over the longer run will be a major new characteristic of this industry in the next decade or two. Cooperation in some areas in the short term, in fact, seems to make continuing competition among a larger number of final assemblers possible in the long term.

Dematurity is also fundamentally changing the nature of the relationship between the car assembler and the component supplier. First, car assemblers are tending to specialize in just that and are withdrawing from component activities. Second, the design and development function, and in many cases the R&D function, is involving the component producers to a much greater extent. More of these activities are now being performed by component firms, and longer-term relationships, along Japanese lines, are essential for this to develop. This involvement in R&D and design and development is particularly relevant for system components where certain larger component suppliers design whole subsystems that are incorporated into the increasingly modularized design of the finished vehicle.

This trend toward systems component suppliers will increase the possibility of some component firms developing an independent and appropriable technological position. This is leading to a situation where companies, like Bosch and Lucas, for example, establish plants in all the main production locations on the basis of their proprietary technology. On the other hand, Japanese firms in such a situation have remained closely tied to their parent car firms within the Japanese group to which they belong (such as the Mitsubishi Group). The ultimate degree of independence will depend on the ownership relationships that evolve.

The trend towards recentralization of the production of major components around each production location is inevitable if the "just-in-time" system is to be fully developed on the Japanese model. Examples of this are the Buick City experiment in the U.S. and the new Japanese plants being built there. At the same time, we have observed that economies of scale of production are coming down in component production, also with new flexible production tooling and plant organization. This facilitates the replication of component production facilities in each of the major production locations. These changes in economies of scale are now relevant for the components industry as the second wave of new investment and plant organization sweeps through it.

Much of the above discussion leads us to conclude that there will not be a wholesale transfer of automobile production to the developing countries. The combination of flexible automation and Japanese advances in production organization have and are continuing to reduce dramatically the number of man-hours required to build a car. Recent estimates conclude that even some of the most promising Third World production sites, such as Korea, have substantially higher production costs than the current world leaders, the Japanese. Similarly, the production of major mechanical components, such as engines and transmissions, require heavy investments in automated tooling, very little relatively highly skilled labor, a very high continuous plant utilization, and no interruptions to the supply to assembly factories abroad. None of these are natural advantages of the developing countries. Also, bulky components are relatively expensive to transport across the globe, and finish components such as trim have to be produced to much higher quality standards than can be achieved in most developing countries. The remaining minor components, such as springs, wiring harnesses, etc., that require manual assembly can currently be sourced in developing countries. However, the automation of subassembly, new materials (such as composite springs), and the importance of minimizing inventory costs and just-in-time delivery are all leading to the relocation of these activities back to the OECD countries.

The Location of Production – the Global
Rebalancing Process

There is no doubt that car production will grow in at least the major developing countries with a large market, prompted by government protectionist measures. Strategies that simply seek to maximize local content in these countries are unlikely to lead to a competitive production base from which to export finished vehicles to sophisticated OECD markets. More imaginative trade-balancing regulations are forcing multinational car firms to locate best-practice plants in those countries if they want to participate in the growing domestic market. A recent example is the transfer of the new Ford plant from Portugal to Mexico. During the next two decades we expect to see only a modest flow of exports from developing countries to OECD countries, mainly in response to such government-multinational bargains. The bulk of Third World production will therefore supply domestic market needs.

What about the location of production within the OECD countries, where a significant productivity gap still exists between Japan and the other OECD countries? We estimated that in 1981 the total number of hours needed to produce a comparable vehicle, including both management and production labor in the final assembler and supplier firms, was around 200 in West Germany and the U.S. and 140 in Japan. This translated into a landed-cost differential of about $2,000 per car with the U.S. and $600 with West Germany (at an exchange rate of ¥215 to the dollar and DM 2.4 to the dollar, respectively). Recent exchange-rate movements have increased the gap with the U.S. and reduced that with West Germany.

This productivity differential has led to a major effort by European and U.S. producers to catch up. Much has already been learned from Japan, and initial investments by the Japanese in Europe and the U.S. in consumer electronics and automobile assembly have demonstrated that much of the Japanese production system is transferable to the West. Indeed, in many ways what the Japanese have done is to rediscover common sense in production organization.

Because each producer is now dependent on selling a considerable portion of its output outside its domestic market, those producers who lag behind have little choice in the medium term but to adopt as much as possible of what have become the newest and best techniques. Efforts by governments to seek to delay this adjustment process, however painful, through protecting their domestic markets will not be sustainable in the long run and may, in fact, make the ultimate adjustment more painful.

On the other hand, modest overall growth in demand in the OECD countries with little access to the growing markets of the developing countries has led to intense competition in all markets. Moreover, the cyclical nature of demand in the OECD countries and the poor macroeconomic prospects and strategic errors by individual producers will inevitably trip up some producers during this process of adjustment. Because of the importance of this industry, governments will be tempted to intervene to prevent their companies from exiting this industry. Indeed, there have now been a number of successful recoveries from very difficult circumstances that encourage the view that, with the right strategy, survival is possible. Austin Rover and Fiat have been turned around in Europe, Chrysler in the U.S., and Mazda in Japan. In addition to being a large employer and a significant element in the balance of payments, this industry is rapidly becoming the major consumer of electronic components and new production technologies such as CAD and robots, and it is once again the key industry through which new managerial practices will be diffused to the rest of the engineering industry.

We have observed three ways in which countries with competitive weaknesses can regain lost ground. These are through straightforward copying of what can be seen in Japan, through collaboration with a Japanese producer in a joint venture, or by observing Japanese producers establishing facilities and demonstrating best practice in the West. Collaboration has been a successful route for some producers (for example, Austin Rover with Honda and General Motors with Toyota) in learning best practice while trading product know-how or market access in return. The demonstration effect of Japanese investment in the West, such as Honda and Nissan in the U.S. and Nissan in the U.K., not only sets a target to be matched by domestic producers but also is most effective in overcoming resistance to making the necessary changes by both management and labor.

From a global perspective, the only possible course, apart from a generalized slide into protectionism and spiraling economic decline as the trading system collapses, is for all producers to be encouraged to level up to new world-best practice as soon as possible. However, this has to be achieved while individual producers are facing enormous uncertainties, and the adjustment process is by no means easy. A successful transition to this rebalanced future—which, as we have already argued, is a bright future—demands sufficient collective understanding that those producers who have achieved a competitive breakthrough have to diffuse their advantages through overseas investment, while those producers who have to adjust must make every effort to do so. The creative breakthrough therefore translates primarily into a change in the balance of ownership of the industry in the OECD countries, not a change in location. Individual governments have to tread a very difficult path between allowing sufficient protection to an ailing domestic producer in order to permit the necessary change in strategy to take effect and, on the other hand, maintaining the competitive pressure on the domestic producer to do so.

The European Perspective

We have already pointed out that Europe's main strength lies in its product technology and design, where it currently dominates the upper and sporting end of the world market. This strength derives from the diversity of the European industry, where there has been no dominant producer or market segment. Different companies have pursued quite different strategies and have accumulated different skills. Thus, Europe has a very rich reservoir of design and product technologies. Moreover, the smaller producers have played an important role in the development of the European industry. The success of the European up-market producers (Daimler Benz, BMW, Audi, Volvo, Saab, Jaguar, and Porsche) in dominating the market for luxury cars in the U.S. is a testament to this. In 1983 the value of 420,000 European exports to the U.S. was $5.3 billion, compared with $10.7 billion earned by the Japanese producers selling 1.86 million vehicles.

This lead in the luxury segment has attracted the attention of both U.S. and Japanese producers, who are targeting future model plans on European-styled up-market vehicles. The European industry will need to continue to push ahead the frontiers of design, packaging, and technology to stay ahead in this area. In this regard, the conservative styling trend that we have seen recently in Europe is worrying. Cars such as the new Volkswagen Golf, BMW 3 and 5 series, and the new Renault 5 may well have to be replaced earlier than expected. Design is a highly transferable commodity, as the flood of Italian-designed Japanese vehicles demonstrates. However, the art of achieving an overall package to meet the best European standards is more difficult and takes a few product generations to perfect.

With hindsight, the European industry was distracted by the desire to mirror the strength of the U.S. producers in having a global production base and by the conviction that this was the only way of establishing a place in the emerging world oligopoly. Volkswagen and Renault have, for different reasons, paid a high price for their efforts to become U.S. producers. Volkswagen has suffered from production and quality problems that used to bedevil the U.S. industry, and Renault has been turned away from a timely renewal of their product range while they established themselves in the U.S. Peugeot is still digesting its acquisition of Chrysler's European operations, and Fiat has pulled back from its global strategy. A second distraction was the attempt to copy Ford in Europe in developing "world cars" with no particular national or producer attributes just as the market was demanding more differentiated products.

The major weakness of the European industry is its persistent overcapacity. Assembly capacity is currently about 12.5 million cars a year, while European demand is only 10.5 million cars, with exports of 1.3 million matched by a similar number of imports from Japan and Eastern Europe. As long as this situation remains, competition in the European market will be cutthroat, which will depress profitability at a time when the European industry needs to invest in new technology and new products and to adjust to the best productivity levels. Despite the belief that European labor is difficult to shed for legal and political reasons, considerable adjustment has gone on in the European industry in recent years. Since 1979, about 150,000 jobs have left the industry in the U.K., 130,000 in Italy, and at least 55,000 in France. In each case these jobs were lost against all the expectations of observers and with little turmoil.

The European industry is always difficult to characterize. Some producers are buoyant at the same time that others are going through difficulties. Unlike in the U.S., the producers in the European industry do not always move up and down in unison. The reversal of the fortunes of the French and Italian industries in the last two years is a case in point. However, it is clear that further capacity reductions will be needed, and producers who have suffered a loss of market share will have to trim their capacity in line with more modest sales targets. This will be accentuated as the Japanese producers establish production facilities in Europe now that all the major markets are closed to further direct imports and exchange rates with the European currencies have moved against the Japanese.

NOTE

*This article is reprinted from the Spring 1985 issue of the *Journal of General Management.* Used by permission of the publisher. Figures 2 and 3 were originally published as figures 6.2 (p. 131) and 6.3 (p. 132) in *The Future of the Automobile: The Report of MIT's International Automobile Program,* codirectors Daniel Roos and Alan Altshuler (Cambridge, MA: The MIT Press, 1984). Used by permission of the publisher.

REFERENCES

Abernathy, W. J. 1978. *The Productivity Dilemma.* Baltimore: John Hopkins University Press.

Clark, R. 1979. *The Japanese Company.* New Haven, CT: Yale University Press.

Dodwell & Co. 1980. *Industrial Groupings in Japan.* Tokyo: Dodwell Marketing Consultants.

Magaziner, I., and M. Hout. 1980. *Japanese Industrial Policy.* London: Policy Studies Institute.

OECD. 1984. *Long Term Perspective of the World Automobile Industry.* Paris.

Ross, Daniel, and Alan Altshuler, codirectors. 1984. *The Future of the Automobile.* Cambridge, MA: The MIT Press.

Schonberger, R. J. 1982. *Japanese Manufacturing Techniques.* New York: Free Press, Macmillan.

Schreiber, J-J. Sevan. 1969. *The American Challenge.* Harmondsworth: Penguin Books.

Seiffert, U., and P. Walzer. 1984. *The Future of Automotive Technology.* London: Frances Pinter.

Sloan, A. P. 1972. *My Years with General Motors.* New York: Anchor Books.

White, M., and M. Trevor. 1983. *Under Japanese Management: The Experiences of British Workers.* London: Heinemann.

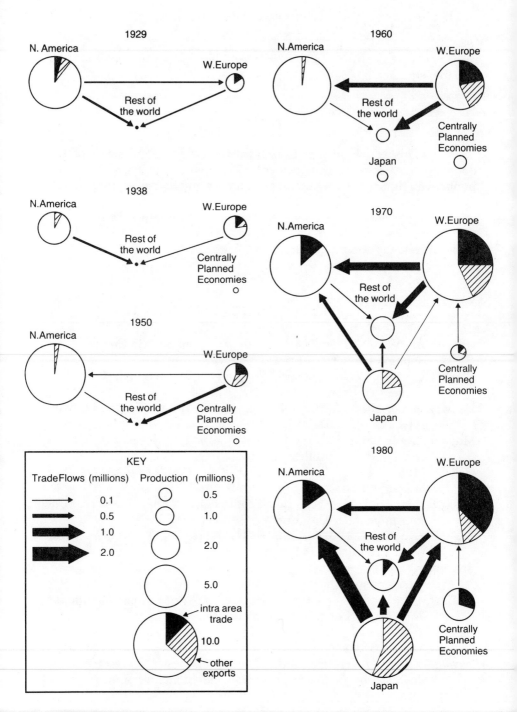

FIGURE 1   World production and trade in automobiles
1929–1980

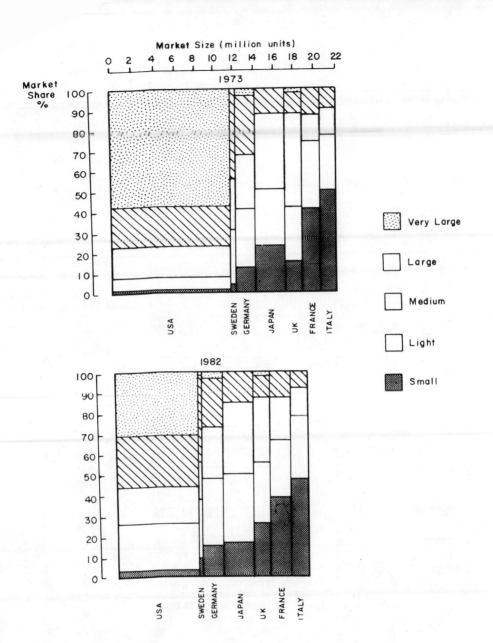

FIGURE 2 The structure of automobile demand in the automobile producing nations

Sources: "SPRU Databank on the Western European Automobile Industry" (1983), *Automotive News Market Data Book*, Ward's MVMA, and *World Motor Data*.

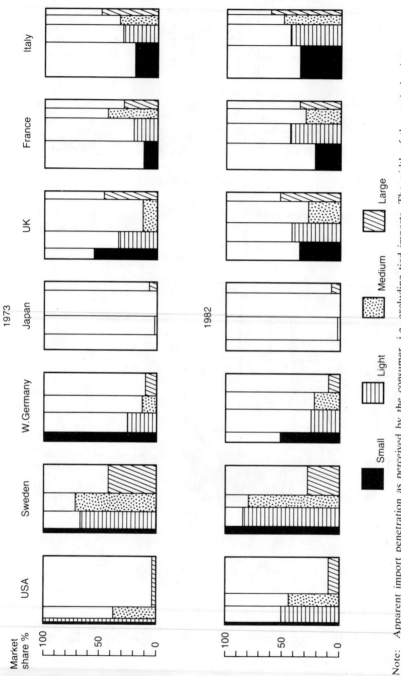

Market share %

1973

USA Sweden W.Germany Japan UK France Italy

1982

Small ■   Light ▥   Medium ⣿   Large ▨

Note: Apparent import penetration as perceived by the consumer, i.e. excluding tied imports. The width of the vertical columns represents the share of the total market accounted for by that size of car, the vertical bar is the share of that market segment held by imports.

FIGURE 3 Import penetration by market segment

Source: See Figure 2.